Escape
from
Mount Moriah

Trials and Triumphs of Making It in the New World

**Featuring an enhanced Introduction
and 10 NEW Chapters**

"told powerfully with charm and wit..."

A Memoir by

JACK ENGELHARD

DayRay Literary Press
British Columbia, Canada

Escape from Mount Moriah:
Trials and Triumphs of Making It in the New World

Library and Archives Canada Cataloguing in Publication
Engelhard, Jack, 1940-, author
Escape from Mount Moriah : trials and triumphs of making it in the new world
/ a memoir by Jack Engelhard. – Third edition.
Issued in print and electronic formats.
ISBN 978-1-77143-096-8 (pbk.).--ISBN 978-1-77143-097-5 (pdf)
1. Engelhard, Jack--Childhood and youth. 2. Jews--Québec (Province)--Montréal--
Biography. 3. Holocaust survivors--Québec (Province)--Montréal--Biography.
4. Montréal (Québec)--Biography. I. Title.
FC2947.26.E54A3 2013   971.4'280049240092   C2013-905942-3

Jack Engelhard may be contacted through: **www.jackengelhard.com**

Cover artwork: screenshot of Jamie Mayers featured in *My Father, Joe*
Short Film Official Selection at the Cannes Film Festival 2011

Previously published in 2001 and 2011 by Comteq Publishing.
Awarded Excellence in Publishing Prize from MPA, 2001.

DayRay Literary Press is a literary imprint
of CCB Publishing: www.ccbpublishing.com

DayRay Literary Press
British Columbia, Canada
www.dayraypress.com

International Bestselling Novelist Jack Engelhard
Author of _Indecent Proposal_

Translated into more than 22 languages and turned into a Paramount motion picture of the same name starring Robert Redford and Demi Moore.

Beautifully written...grittily honest...
delightfully charming...

Readers have spoken. They wanted more from this masterpiece. So 10 new chapters have been added in what many cite as among the finest coming-of-age memoir ever written. Legendary novelist Jack Engelhard (_Indecent Proposal_) recovers the past with fresh gems in this award-winning book, honored, later in film, for its unique, minimalist style that delivers absolute brilliance. Each short chapter sparkles and shines in this little memoir that could.

Torn from their homes in France at the onset of the Nazi invasion, and after a harrowing escape across the Pyrenees, the Engelhard family -- Noah, Ida, Sarah and Jack -- must begin lives as refugees in a new world -- first Canada (Montreal), later the United States. The experiences that shaped young Jack Engelhard were those that profoundly changed the world. Engelhard, often likened to Hemingway and James M. Cain for precision, helps us understand that life itself is the process of learning who you are.

Featuring an enhanced Introduction
and 10 NEW Chapters
starting on page 93

Includes the story "My Father, Joe"
Short Film Official Selection at the
Cannes Film Festival

Praise received for *Escape from Mount Moriah*

"In *Escape from Mount Moriah*, Jack Engelhard achieves the impossible. In a single story, a single page, a single paragraph, even a single sentence, he combines a deep, abiding love with the unvarnished, penetrating gaze of the past, gritty realism with sublime philosophy, brevity with depth, the quintessentially Jewish with the essentially universal, and witty humor with the utmost seriousness."
- Nissan Ratzlav-Katz, former Opinion Editor for
Israel National News.com, is a marketing and business writer providing services for a wide array of global organizations

"For my money every one of the 28 stories in this memoir has a latent brilliance and character unmatched in any published stories of their kind. Jack Engelhard is the last of the Hemingways."
- John W. Cassell, author of *Crossroads: 1969*

"The adventurous, humorous, sometimes wonderfully strange exploits of a youth during his family's adjustment to a new world, these compelling boyhood memories are of an almost Tom Sawyer character, albeit with ironic Yiddish twists.

With themes of humiliation, intimidation, and alienation, this powerful book illustrates how the Holocaust did not end in 1945, but continued to reverberate through successive decades, even until the present day."
- Chris Leppek, *Jewish News* (Denver)

"This book is a winner within its own niche of brilliance...to the child in us, living eternally. Engelhard's balsamic bible of a book."
- Linda Shelnutt

Also by Jack Engelhard

Indecent Proposal: Fiction.
Translated into more than 22 languages and turned into
a Paramount motion picture of the same name starring
Robert Redford and Demi Moore.

Compulsive: A Novel: Fiction.

Slot Attendant: A Novel about a Novelist. Fiction.

The Girls of Cincinnati: Fiction.

The Prince of Dice: Fiction.

The Bathsheba Deadline: Fiction.

The Horsemen: Non-fiction.
Excerpted in *The New York Times*

The Days of the Bitter End: Fiction.

* * * * *

A new Spanish language edition of *Indecent Proposal*
was released in 2013 in both print and e-book editions
and made available for purchase worldwide.

The author wishes to express his gratitude and thanks
to translator Frederick Martin-Del-Campo for his fine
work in this and other projects.

<u>Praise received for Jack Engelhard's other books</u>:

"Precise, almost clinical language...Is this book fun to read? You betcha."
- *The New York Times,* for *Indecent Proposal*

"Well-wrought characters, exhilarating pace...funny and gruff...a fast and well-crafted book."
- *Philadelphia Inquirer,* for *Indecent Proposal*

"*Compulsive* is enormously enjoyable, and so easy to get into."
- Kenneth Slawenski, (Random House) bestselling author of *J.D. Salinger: A Life* - www.deadcaulfields.com

"Engelhard tells the story of *The Girls of Cincinnati* with precision through his masterful narration. Every word has a place and every page has a quote you will want to remember."
- Lois Sack, author of *Her Brightness in the Darkness*

"A towering literary achievement."
- Letha Hadady, author, for *The Bathsheba Deadline*

"Savor it...it may be the best, sharpest, most vivid portrait of life around the racetrack ever written."
- Ray Kerrison, *New York Post* columnist
writing for the *National Star,* for *The Horsemen*

"It is such a fantastic read that I wonder, can any reviewer ever do it justice."
- Gisela Hausmann, author and blogger,
for *Slot Attendant: A Novel About a Novelist*

"What a great story. If you missed the 60s – if you missed the excitement, the passion, the radicalism, the thrills, the hopes and dreams – this book brings it all alive. I could not put it down."
- Kmgroup review for *The Days of the Bitter End*

Dedicated to
Leslie, David, Rachel, Sarah, Toni...and Siena!

...and to the loving memory of my parents
Noah and Ida

Immeasurable gratitude to
Jeffrey Farkas, John W. Cassell, Linda Shelnutt

Special thanks and gratitude to the late great book reviewer of *The Philadelphia Inquirer*, Dave Appel, for his encouragement to stop talking these stories and get them down in writing.

Contents

Preface

A Note About Nu Nu Nu

In these pages, the lament nu nu nu is sometimes used by my father. Let me explain.

Nu Nu Nu is impossible to translate into English -- just as it is impossible to translate a sigh or a shrug. Nu nu nu is the eternal Yiddish answer, the ultimate resignation that says, "The rest is up to God."

But even God said nu nu nu, or words to that effect. On the Sixth Day He said to the angels, "Let us make man."

Moses, when preparing to write these words from God's dictation, protested, saying, "That's all the scoffers need. The entire Torah is an expression of Your Oneness, and here You say we? They'll say, 'God shares His powers? God needs help?' They're certain to misunderstand."

And God answered him: "If they choose to misunderstand, let them misunderstand."

That was the first instance of nu nu nu -- God saying, "The rest is up to man."

Along with the Torah, Moses carried down nu nu nu from Mount Sinai and passed it along to his people for everlasting. But it is not an expression of hopeless resignation. It is an expression of hopeful resignation. Sometimes, yes, it is a mixture of both. The question may be asked; how can people feel hopeful and hopeless at the same time?

The answer is this; Nu nu nu.

1

My Father, Joe

Now we had it good. Six million never made it out. We...we escaped France when the Nazis and their gendarmes were beginning their roundups in our district in Toulouse. We walked the Pyrenees...hid in Spain...rested in Portugal...and found refuge in Montreal, Canada -- much later we moved to America.

Amazing how so much can be summed up in a single paragraph, and life, as we know, is not lived by the paragraph. Take my word for it that our escape was a tremendous adventure -- two years of running, evading, a hundred close calls in cars, trains, ships, a thousand moments of doubt, fear, helplessness, and being spooked at every turn by the sights and sounds of Nazi boots.

But I won't go into all that -- that's another book, and frankly, it's a story that's already been written by others -- even cheapened and trivialized and, to tell the truth, unless you lived it you'll never know. But

1

maybe I can share with you what it was like being a refugee.

As for my father, and so much about this is about my father, let me say that he was no ordinary man. He was a man of great learning. He knew Torah and Talmud from end to end, all of which had been crammed into him as a Yeshiva-boy in Poland. He was also a man of action. When he found out that we were on "The List" no words of caution from my mother could detain him. He knew just what to do…

* * *

Now here we were in Montreal.

My father was a businessman. Like Rockefeller was a rabbi, so was my father a businessman. He tottered from failure to failure, but with pride. He was his own man.

He used to say, "I don't know what it is with me. I can't work for another man." This was no weakness in his eyes. No, it was strength. A sign of character.

To which my mother would say, "Yes, a character you are."

But, for a spell, my father did work for another man, and Mr. Snow was his name.

Mr. Snow was a handbag manufacturer. He had a factory on St. Lawrence Street where he employed 25

2

workers -- designers, cutters, and sewers. In Europe, my father had had a factory of 40 workers -- or 50, or 60, or maybe 100.

The number grew along with my father's wrath, for he did not like working for Mr. Snow. So he'd come home and say, "He calls himself a fabricant? I had a factory of 50 and he's going to teach me about handbags?" The next day it was a factory of 60, and so on.

My father was a designer for Mr. Snow. Father designed handbags with frames, following the classic European fashion and the style that had made him revered in the trade. Now he'd bring home his designs for my mother's review...designs which Mr. Snow had rejected again and again.

Mr. Snow, you see, had no faith in handbags with frames.

Frames were out.

Zippers were in.

"Zippers," my father said.

In time, though, he stopped being contemptuous... and, he stopped bringing home his designs.

Gradually, he fell into his great trancelike silences.

Mother would ask him how things were going in the factory and he'd say, "Good enough." She'd ask him why he stopped bringing home his samples. He'd respond by staring off in the distance, and I never knew what he saw there, except Abraham, Isaac and Jacob. He lived more in their world than in his own.

Naturally, one day he forgot his lunch bag.

"Go bring this to your father," my mother said.

I walked past the St. Lawrence Street grocery stores, butcher shops (Kosher-Bosher), bakeries and everything that was retail and wholesale. Further up, factories had been turned into tenements, tenements into factories, and in such a place, warped from top to bottom, worked my father.

Approaching the landing you could hear the roar of the sewing machines. Closer, you smelled the adhesives and the leather. Inside, I did not know where to begin. Cutters were bent over huge tables slicing up giant stretches of animal hides. Sewers were grinding in frenzy, never once gazing up, as though somewhere in their urgency of livelihood they had lost the human sense of wonder and curiosity.

For the most part, these were Jewish refugees who were paid by the piece. But the rush of their machines were like wails. These people were in a hurry to forget the past and catch up to the present.

The designers -- the nobility of a handbag factory -- where were they? There I'd find my father.

I stepped into the back room where rough-talking characters were packing finished handbags

4

into cardboard boxes. These types had a look and a word for everybody.

I heard them yell, "Joe, Joe, where's my Coke?" Then they'd laugh.

There must be an errand boy here, I thought, named Joe. Every place has a Joe.

I heard others in the factory take up the same chant. "Joe, Joe, where's my Coke?"

This Joe, some joke he must be.

Then I saw my father. He was carrying a tray of Cokes, but not moving fast enough.

"Over here, Joe. Atta boy."

How, I wondered, does a man go from Noah ben Jacob to Joe?

My father would have had the answer...but I would never ask.

Escape from Mount Moriah

2

Penn Station

Mother was hard of hearing, so she never picked up English, even after years living in Montreal.

Not everybody believed her, by the way. Years later my cousin Roma said, "She hears what she wants to hear."

The problem, as my mother saw it, wasn't hers.

She used to say, "Let them learn Yiddish."

My father had read Dickens in the original back in France, so he was something of an English expert. In actuality, he was very poor when it came to the spoken language, but compared to my mother he was Winston Churchill.

"Penn Station," he said to her one day.

My mother, for some reason, was traveling to New York and I was going along. I had no idea why.

Didn't know then and still don't know today the reason for that week's trip.

So my father told my mother that when she got there -- to New York -- she was to get in a cab and tell the driver, "Penn Station."

Not "Pennsylvania Station," my father warned her. Only people from another city said, "Pennsylvania Station" -- and that's all the cab driver had to know to take you for a nice tour around the entire city -- with the meter running.

"Moreover," said my father, "don't say another word." One word besides "Penn Station" would reveal her accent and betray her as being from another country. That guaranteed a tour around the city twice.

Now, "Penn Station" anybody can say and still sound like an American.

"Say Penn Station," said my father.

"Penn Station," said my mother.

"Very good."

Each day my father tested her. "Penn Station," said my mother.

"And what if the driver asks you a question?"

"I say nothing."

"What if he asks you if you like the weather? What do you say?"

"Penn Station."

Penn Station -- perhaps the only two words in the entire English language that cannot be mispronounced.

So, with those words, we traveled to New York by train, which took us to Grand Central Station. I had never been to America before and never seen so many people under the same roof. There was no end to the crowds, or the building. There were doors everywhere, but they only led to more doors. Was there an outside? Or was this America from beginning to end? We were lost.

Finally, we found the right crowd and found ourselves out in the open. Remarkably, people, here in America, didn't have to whisper. They could walk and talk and shout and there were no police or even secret police to stop them or make them afraid. Taxis were lined up against the curb. My mother wanted a Jewish face for a driver but, in New York, every face is Jewish.

"Here lady," someone said, and just like that, we were in a cab.

"Penn Station," said my mother.

I knew what she was thinking. The driver might ask, "Which Penn Station? Why Penn Station?"

But he asked no questions. He flipped the meter handle and started the drive.

My mother was worried. Had she said "Penn Station" properly? Already we were riding too long, it seemed, and I could sense my mother wanting to protest. But what could she say except Penn Station again, and my father had warned her against pushing her luck.

"Say it once," he had said. "Only once."

So...she had said it once, and like God who had brought the world into being merely by saying the words -- behold, here was Penn Station!

"Penn Station," said the driver.

"Yes," said my mother, chancing the extra English word now that she was safely here...and, feeling a bit extravagant.

3

Moishe, The War Hero

A man named Moishe moved next to us on St. Urbain Street and on hot summer nights, eating grapes and cherries on his second-floor landing, he used to thrill me with stories about Israel. His exploits against the Arabs in the war of 1948 -- still fresh in the early 1950s -- were of the measure of King David's.

"So there I was," he said, "surrounded by Arabs. Arabs to the left. Arabs to the right. Arabs in front. Arabs in back. Hundreds of them, prepared to kill. Who was in the middle? Me. Well..."

Naturally, he vanquished them all -- all by himself.

I was not surprised. The whole story about how we won Israel was a miracle. There had to be hundreds of people like Moishe to beat back the thousands of Arabs.

And Moishe looked the type. There was a pioneer roughness about him. He seemed as wild as the Judaean Hills and in his eyes you could see the vastness of Sinai.

I envied him. I wanted to be like him. The new Jew.

We had a schedule. Each night after supper I'd join him on the landing and start by saying, "Tell me..."

"Well, once an Arab had me against a wall with a bayonet. Let me tell you..."

Of course, Moishe prevailed. All his stories had a happy ending. After all, he was here, wasn't he?

Incredible, I thought, that while we pale-faced Jews were fleeing the Nazis, in another part of the world a Biblical romance was taking place. A different kind of Jew was fighting -- and winning.

The names alone entranced me. Instead of Bergen-Belsen, Auschwitz, Treblinka, I heard Palmach, Irgun, Hagannah.

How was it, I thought, that my Jews never won a battle...and Moishe's Jews never lost a battle? My Jews were great in Torah...his were glorious in war.

I remember being taught how virtuous it was not to fight back. Yet standing obediently in line for the ovens -- mothers and their children by the hundreds, thousands and finally the millions -- this was so virtuous?

"One time," Moishe said, "there I was in an alley. I was out of bullets. Only a knife to my name. Well, twenty Arabs had me encircled. What should I do? Should I run? Or..."

No, Moishe wouldn't run.

Moishe wouldn't lie, either.

One night I went to visit him and he wasn't home. His wife told me a strange thing. She said he was a good talker, her Moishe. He'd come straight from the concentration camp here to Montreal. He'd never been to Israel, she said.

Of course, I didn't believe her.

Escape from Mount Moriah

4

Fish

My father came from a small town in Poland where everything besides work and study was superfluous.

By study I mean Torah...sometimes 15 hours a day!

Father had been the classic Yeshiva boy -- long earlocks dangling over the books.

Later in France, and now here in Montreal of course, he was clean shaven. But, as my mother used to remind him, "You can leave Prochnik, but Prochnik can't leave you."

If to Solomon all was vanity (or futility), to my father all was excess.

My father's father had been a very pious man. So pious that -- wealthy though he was by Prochnik standards -- he slept on a board of wood rather than in bed. This was his way of shunning excess and saving the rewards of comfort for the-world-to-come.

Father came from that mold.

One day in Montreal we went to visit the Sterns. They had come over on the boat with us. My father was still struggling. Mr. Stern was making a fine living and beginning to think he was "American."

Mr. Stern showed my father his fishbowl.

"Look," said Mr. Stern.

My father looked and there, inside the fishbowl, he saw gold fish, yellow fish, blue fish, red fish, green fish, white fish and silver fish all swimming back and forth, as fish do.

Mr. Stern was very proud of these fish.

Somehow they made him a man of property, a man of leisure. No more greenhorn.

My father only saw fish -- and fish, as a hobby, did not thrill him much.

"What do you think?" asked Mr. Stern.

"What's to think?" said my father.

"What do you think of my fish?"

"A fish is a fish."

This devastated Mr. Stern.

"These aren't just fish," protested Mr. Stern.

"So what are they?"

"They're special fish."

"How are they so special?"

Mr. Stern grew irritable. "They swim," he proclaimed.

"This," said my father, "makes a fish special?"

"I WATCH them swim," said Mr. Stern.

This amazed my father.

He said, "This is what you do with your time? You watch fish swim?"

"Yes."

"All day?"

"Not all day. When I come home from work. It's very relaxing for a man."

For a man such as my father, relaxing was a glass of tea and a newspaper. Not fish.

He said, "When you come home from work you watch fish swim? You have nothing better to do?"

"So what do YOU do with your spare time?"

Here Mr. Stern had my father. My father had no spare time. Not only that, he could not fathom the concept. Spare time? When there was endless work to be done...and the Torah to be gone over again and again? There were seventy different meanings and shadings to each word of the Torah. What spare time could there be?

"Nu, Nu, Nu," said my father with a Prochnik shrug. "If I had spare time, maybe even I would watch fish swim."

This was his attempt at harmony, but the visit had not been a success. My mother later said to my father, "You had to make such a business about his fish?"

My father kept his silence, but for days -- even weeks afterward -- he was still puzzled.

"A grown man," he'd mutter, "and this is what he does. He watches fish swim."

)

The Sewing Machine

The Mahlers were strange people, which would not have bothered me except that we lived with them.

There was Mr. Mahler, who hardly ever said a word. Mrs. Mahler was a hunchback. The two kids were cute and wonderful, but then there was their uncle, Mr. Mahler's brother -- and Hershel was his name.

But Hershel came later.

From the start there was tension. Here we were, a family of four, occupying a single room on St. Urbain Street. The rest of the house belonged to the Schwartz's, who one day moved out. The Mahler's moved in -- and there we were. They could have thrown us out, but they didn't. Not right away.

They were refugees themselves, greener, in fact, than we were. We'd already been in Montreal since the mid-1940s and they'd just arrived from France. There they had tarried after the war. Both Mr. and Mrs. Mahler had death camp tattoo marks on their arms.

I had no notion what they'd endured, but Mrs. Mahler carried herself well. I was a bit in love with her.

Yes, there was that terrible affliction on her back, but her cheerfulness and good nature were so forceful that you saw nothing but her radiant face.

She was French in all the right ways. As we became familiar, she'd be offended if I did not kiss her first when I got home from school. Always at that time she had milk and chocolates prepared for me, and hunchback or not, she had a French eye. She told me that the boy next door was handsome. I sulked. She said, "But of course you are much more handsome."

Her husband -- who knew what made him what he was? Silence was all I ever knew of him. He was tall, slow-moving, and his face was long, sad and hollow in the manner of Abraham Lincoln. I sensed great tragedy in him, a man raging inside from a gathering of secrets.

I was never quite sure whether we were one of his secrets. What were we doing in his house? Did he ask for us? But here we were, and possibly he resented the fact of our presence. Or maybe not. Certainly and emphatically he ignored us, but I cannot say we were the root of his haughty indignation. He had no friends other than his radio. This -- a big black standing box in the living room -- he listened to all evening, turning the knobs back and forth.

We all shared the same bathroom, and we managed. My mother and Mrs. Mahler shared the same kitchen, and she managed. When it came to sharing other peoples' homes, my mother had become a professional. When conflicts arose it was she, my mother, who yielded.

There was peace between our two families but, as my mother used to say, "We are Hitler's children." This made us the heirs of wrath and, with the Nazis gone (at least in those uniforms), we had it mostly upon ourselves to practice vengeance.

Now, as with all things good or bad, Hershel came upon us unexpectedly. We did not even know that Mr. Mahler had a brother, but one day here he came, here he was, and here he stayed. He was a short, dark man with busy movements. Yes, busy was the word for Hershel.

Though I kept no books on him, it's possible to say he worked eighteen hours a day, seven days a week. Where? In a closet that he turned into a workroom. Was he happy working in such confinement? Of course not. He wanted our room, which he'd had his eyes on from the start.

In fact, he was not a shy man at all.

When he first us, that day he walked in with his sewing machine, he said, "Who are these people?"

Did I say sewing machine? Of course, because this was the beginning and end of it all.

In case I forgot to mention it, Hershel was a tailor -- or something. He did piecework for large clothing manufacturers, and his dream was to make enough money to build his own factory.

Thus he sewed morning to midnight on a Singer machine that roared even for the dead. For the living, like ourselves, the din pierced every thought and shattered body and soul. We woke up and went to bed to the thunder of Hershel's machine.

Did my parents complain?

First of all, we were here at their mercy, so we were in no position to complain.

Second, as my father used to say -- quoting the Sages:

Why should any man complain? It's enough that he's alive.

Third, my parents admired Hershel. What was greater than earning a living?

So my father and mother did not begrudge Hershel and his sewing machine.

The neighbors were another story. They were not happy about the relentless noise. They never said so to us in words, but their looks spoke their minds.

As for Hershel, he was impervious to everything. It seemed as though he wanted to drive everybody out -- family, neighbors -- but most of all -- us.

"If they don't like it," I once heard him say to his brother, "let them go. Let them go."

Yes, he wanted us to go. He wanted our room.

We did not leave for this reason: the rent was low. We could not afford another place. Moving itself -- even to another room in another house -- might cost twenty dollars. Who had twenty dollars? A security payment might cost fifty dollars. Who had fifty dollars? So we stayed.

One day I came home from school and the house was empty. Where were my milk and chocolates? Where was Mrs. Mahler? Come to think of it, where was the roaring ear-splitting noise from the sewing machine?

My parents, I found in the room, ashen from fright.

Something terrible had happened. The police, said my father -- my mother was too grief-stricken to speak -- had come and confiscated Hershel's sewing machine.

This is so terrible? I thought.

But yes it was because Hershel -- and through Hershel's accusation, the Mahlers as well -- were holding us as the informers.

"God forbid," said my mother, "that we should confiscate a man's livelihood."

They spoke in whispers. An arrangement had been made. So long as my parents stayed in the room they'd remain unharmed. If they stepped out, anything might happen. That went for me, too. The Mahlers, meanwhile, were in the kitchen brooding, mourning the sewing machine that was the source of their living, for as it turned out, that's what sustained them all.

My mother said that immediately after the sewing machine had been taken away, Mrs. Mahler came after her with a knife.

Mrs. Mahler?

Hershel had said, according to her, "Kill her!"

"In the end," said my father, "everything comes home. Even lies." Which I didn't understand.

But this I understood. We were as if in prison. We could not leave the room for food, air, or even the bathroom. I had come in during some sort of lapse. Because Hershel had threatened to strangle the first one of us he saw.

Mr. Mahler? He had said nothing. Yet because of that silence we feared him most of all. Hershel the big talker would probably do nothing. But Mr. Mahler -- he was like stillness before lightning.

I felt an urge to protest and be a hero by means of going out and pleading our innocence, especially before Mrs. Mahler. I could not have lost her affection over the turn of a single event -- an event so false.

But no plea of mine, said my father, would be heard.

The hatred and violence were already cast. Tale-bearing, he said, was one of the greatest evils of our people. So costly had betrayal been to our people, from Moses' time through Roman times, that a curse was pronounced against talebearers even in our 18 Benedictions. Once accused of that sin, there was no forgiveness.

The untruth of this, the injustice of this accusation against my father and mother, overwhelmed my pity for the Mahlers. Not for a moment did I think of their straits when our predicament was so pressing. In the other room, people were plotting, and waiting for us with knives.

We slept fitfully that night, with full bladders. In the morning I was not sent to school. My father did not leave for work. My mother stayed put. No food. The Mahlers were still in the kitchen. Not even up in the Pyrenees, with Nazis potentially behind every bush, did we know such fear.

Yet we were in a time of peace, among our own people.

How, I wondered, do things get so twisted?

"Why," I asked my father again and again, "don't you just tell them it was the neighbors? Tell them the truth."

"They don't want to hear," he said.

He knew false accusation...that it had shape, breath and life.

He said false accusation was a demon. Like all demons it was formed by God on the Sixth Day of creation. But before He could complete the demon came the Seventh Day -- the Sabbath -- and God rested. So for evermore the demon remained unfinished.

So this! Unfinished...and so it would remain.

My mother made the first and last attempt at peace. She stepped out to go to the bathroom. Mr. Mahler blocked her path.

"Quickly turn back for the sake of your life," he said.

My father ran out to rescue her. "What are you doing?" he asked her, and walked her back.

That evening we packed our suitcases and in the middle of the night escaped with our belongings. But as for me, there was no counting or measuring all that we had left behind.

6

Relatives from America

This was big news. My Uncle Harry and Aunt Jennie were coming in from New York to visit us in Montreal.

Though they were from my father's side, it was my mother who was truly thrilled. To my father, family was nothing. To my mother, family was everything. She told me, "They're your own blood."

This was important to me because other than my parents and my sister, I had no relatives. Those we'd left behind in France as we fled the Nazis were nothing but vanishing memory. After all, I was four when we escaped.

Here in Montreal I grew envious each time a classmate mentioned a visit from an aunt...uncle... grandmother...cousin. Where were mine?

Finally, I'd get to see what an aunt and uncle looked like. From New York yet. "Yes," said my father, "they are very, very wealthy."

Oh yes!

Of course, Father had grown up with Harry in Prochnik, Poland. But Harry had left for America even before the Second World War -- and made a fortune in the publishing business.

Uncle Harry was an American through and through.

In preparation for the visit, my mother scrubbed and polished the entire house.

We lived on Esplanade then, and it was one of the few times we occupied an entire house -- but, not so fast. We were actually boarders -- as always -- except that the landlord was a bachelor who needed but a single room. This was no generosity on his part. He saw us as caretakers -- specifically my mother. He regarded her as his maid. He used to leave cigar ashes on his armoire to make sure she was cleaning up after him properly.

He owned a prosperous beauty parlor on Park Avenue, but he would not allow me to use his radio even for a minute. When he came home late at night he'd place his hand on the radio to test whether it was warm from use.

Once when we were all in bed with colds and being cared for by my mother, the landlord came in and said, "What is this! A hospital?"

So this made us poor relatives for my Uncle Harry and Aunt Jennie. But my mother was resolved to make us worthy, so she bought me new clothes just for them. I used to hate to try on new clothes, but this was different. This was for my Uncle Harry...Aunt Jennie.

Without even knowing them, I loved them. I imagined what it would be like seeing them for the first time. I was even worried about an excess of emotion -- all the hugs and kisses, and tears from that yearning across continents and generations.

Safe in America, Uncle Harry must have been worried sick about how his older brother was faring in Europe under the boot of Cossacks and Nazis.

But my father not only survived the Nazis, he had been fruitful and multiplied...a wife, a daughter, a son. What gifts to show a brother! Poor we were, but only in money -- and surely Uncle Harry would be gratified. Uncle Harry...as the time of his visit grew closer, I built him up in my mind and gave him the face of benevolence.

Everything was ready that day. It was summer. I was spiffed out. I declined a game of street baseball with Doodie, Velvel, and the gang so as not to soil myself and, anyway, all I wanted to do was wait.

And so I waited until...here came a sparkling blue car, slowed down, and parked in front of the house. I checked and, yes, New York license plates. The sight of that alone stirred me. They were parking illegally, in front of a fire hydrant, but who could bother them? They were Americans. My aunt and uncle.

All of Esplanade was alert, watching. This was a street where your business was everybody's business. In fact, when my sister left the house with a date on Saturdays, up and down the block windows opened and heads nodded or turned. So it was now. A car from America was here, on Esplanade.

But why weren't they coming out, Uncle Harry and Aunt Jennie? They were fixed in the car. After minutes turned into at least half an hour, my smile began to fade. Were they disappointed in what they were seeing? Was Esplanade not fit for them? Were they thinking to turn back?

But finally, out they came, and as for Uncle Harry in particular, yes, he sure did look like an American...so robust. Who but an American had that look -- this look that said he owned the world.

This American was my uncle, my blood, and I wasted no time. Even before he slammed shut his car door I was upon him. I jumped on him and clung by his neck. Now it was his turn. He would clasp me to his heart and circle me around like the Torah itself.

Instead, he tore me loose, tentacle by tentacle, as a man who'd had a nightlong struggle with an octopus.

When he finally had me free, he flung me to the ground.

And that was that.

Escape from Mount Moriah

7

A Month in St. Agathe

St. Agathe was a resort for the rich. (Though, really, is there a resort for the poor?) Year-round it was a French-Canadian village set high in the Laurentian Mountains, about 40 miles outside of Montreal. In the summer, rich families from Montreal vacationed in St. Agathe. So what were we doing there? Good question.

First, let me remind you that in France, before the war, my parents had been rich. Summer after summer my father sent us off on vacation. On weekends he'd visit, as was the custom among our class.

So why should it be different in Montreal?

Because in Montreal we had no money.

Yet a small thing like that did not stop my father from sending me and my mother off to St. Agathe. Weren't we as good as the rest? If not, we'd show them anyhow. The "show" -- this was important.

There was even a way of measuring how well a man had succeeded in the new country.

To spend a week in St. Agathe was a sign to your countrymen that you were doing okay. Two weeks in St. Agathe and you were doing very well. Three weeks in St. Agathe meant you were getting up there with the Gewertzes and the Bronfmans. A month in St. Agathe? You must BE a Gewertz or a Bronfman.

My father said he'd visit us on weekends. So my mother found a nice place by a lake. A French-Canadian family owned the house. In the summer they rented rooms to vacationers like ourselves -- rich people from Montreal.

Everything was beautiful. The house...the lake...the people. St. Agathe was beautiful. Sparkling hotels were arranged around the lake like diamonds. In the daytime, red boats sailed by. At night, there was music from the hotel ballrooms.

Farther off, at the edge of town, was the railroad station -- my favorite place. I used to wait for trains. I used to watch them curl down the mountain and catch a thrill when they roared in.

Once a week, on Fridays, my mother came along with me to the train station to wait for my father. He was supposed to come on the 6:28. That first Friday, though, he did not show up.

Was my mother alarmed? No. She called him. He said he could not make it because of business, but he'd be here next Friday. "Good," said my mother. "But where is the money?"

"On its way," said my father. "The money is in the mail."

So the next morning we walked to the post office. There was money there, but not for us.

As we walked along the beautiful streets of beautiful St. Agathe, my mother said, "We have no money."

No money for the rent of our vacation apartment. No money even for food.

"So let's go back to Montreal," I said.

"Didn't I just tell you? We have no money."

No money even to get back to Montreal.

Back in our room we heard music from the hotel ballrooms.

My mother told me, "When I was a girl, I used to dance."

The next day she sent me to the railroad station for another purpose. We needed toilet paper.

I went there every day to steal as much as I could.

But food I did not steal.

So we starved.

Not completely, of course, because my mother borrowed bread and butter from the Pleuffs, the people who owned the boarding house. They must have guessed we weren't too rich, to be borrowing bread and butter -- plus not paying the rent.

"When my husband comes..." my mother kept assuring the Pleuffs.

But the 6:28 arrived, and again without my father. So again my mother phoned him.

"Business," he said.

Next week he'd be here for sure.

"Money," said my mother. "We need money."

Now she was alarmed.

He'd already sent the money by telegraph, my father said.

So we walked to the telegraph office...and there was no money.

The Pleuffs finally refused us bread and butter and allowed my mother one last phone call. This was what my father had to say: The reason he had sent no money was because he had no money. For the same reason he could not come to St. Agathe.

And for the same reason we could not leave St. Agathe.

"Something has to change," said my mother. "Either you come here or we go there."

"Wait another week," said my father.

"A week? We can't last the day," said my mother. "We have no food."

So I got a job as a baker's helper and earned enough money to get us back to Montreal, where my mother caused some envy among her rich friends by telling them the truth -- that she'd spent a MONTH in St. Agathe.

Escape from Mount Moriah

8

My First World Series

Canada has a reputation for being cold, yet I remember summer days in Montreal when there was nothing to do but sweat. Sometimes, it seemed, the city came to a stop. If you listened you could hear the clunk of a baseball bat against pavement -- but not much more.

One such day -- I don't remember the year, but it must have been the early 1950s -- I meandered up Fairmount Street for no other purpose than to be out of the house. At worst, I'd stop in at Abe's, and for a quarter, get me a nice thick milkshake.

But a new candy, news, and soda shop had opened directly across from Abe's. The store did a good business, mainly because of the owner's daughter. She worked behind the counter and was some eyeful. She was a beautiful and sexy lady. She had pitch black hair and wore a nurse's tunic. She had large, ripe, upright breasts, and the reason I noticed was because...who couldn't?

She was always leaning across the counter, sharing whispers with the older guys. There was laughter. I never knew the joke.

I used to observe this from the outside. One day I decided to go in.

The daughter was there behind the counter, but down the other end exchanging the usual secrets with two guys who wore white suits and black shirts. One of them was twirling a long keychain. I sat down at the counter, but it was as though I were invisible. I did not have the courage to demand service. I was just a kid. I had the feeling that I was not necessary here -- but even then, I was a person of extremes. I figure people who do not love me hate me.

But right in front of me was a television set, and this was good. Better yet, a baseball game was on. Not just any baseball game...the World Series. I thought, never mind the milkshake. Instead, I'd get to watch my first World Series. That, I concluded, was how I'd spend the afternoon -- and it seemed quite wonderful.

I watched a couple of innings and was very much caught up in the game when the guy with the keychain said, "It's hot out here. Let's go in back."

The other guy said, "Let's bring the TV."

"But the kid's watching it," the daughter said...and then she giggled when one of them whispered to her.

Mr. Keychain walked over, unplugged the set, and carried it off. Then they all disappeared into the back. I waited a few minutes, as if something might still happen. But what could happen?

So I got up and left. Outside it was still very hot.

Escape from Mount Moriah

9

I Resign

My first job was with a man named Mr. Cohen, who ran a nursery. When I first went out there, to Cote de Neige in the vast outskirts of Montreal, I thought I'd be working with children. These turned out to be plants.

The job required being on your knees all morning and afternoon to pull out weeds, row after row under a spiteful July and then August sun.

The weeds grew fast. One day I counted them, how many I was pulling, and the total came to 6,740. They grew tall and thick and you never knew what lurked between them. Rats, for example. Rats bigger than dogs. One afternoon there I was, face to face with a rat. He stayed. I ran.

I told Mr. Cohen about it and he laughed.

As for me, I did not think it so funny. I was about 14 then. Most boys my age were delivering newspapers -- but we needed more money.

So each day for a good part of that summer I took three streetcars to Cote de Neige and three streetcars back, an hour and a half in the morning, an hour and a half at night, and in between I pulled weeds.

Now, the thirst was the worst of it; no matter how much water you drank, it was never enough. The walk from Mr. Cohen's nursery to the first streetcar stop was about two miles, and I walked this distance filthy from dust and empty from thirst. I passed beautiful, new suburban homes -- another life for me. People would be sitting outside on their lawns, watering the grass.

What a waste of water, I thought. What were they watering anyway? Weeds?

Or they'd be eating juicy watermelon.

Now, I know this is what I saw. I once saw Maurice Richard sitting outside just like that, eating watermelon. Maurice Richard, the Babe Ruth of hockey. I never even told my friends about this. First, nobody sees God...so how can you see Maurice Richard? Second, this was mine. I wanted to keep it to myself.

I did tell Mr. Cohen about it and he laughed.

I hated this job very much.

One day Mr. Cohen asked me to run a hose over a long row of flowers. "I'm promoting you," he said with a chuckle. Accidentally, I aimed the hose in his direction and drenched him from head to toe. I missed no part of him.

"I needed a shower anyway," he said.

I said to myself, I am not long for this job.

One more rat, I promised myself, and I am gone for good. Goodbye.

Only a few days later, nearing the end of August and the beginning of school, here was that rat standing between me and a weed I was about to extract. I fled to Mr. Cohen's office. Before stepping in, I took time to collect myself.

Then I said, "Mr. Cohen, can I talk to you for a minute?"

"Even two," he said.

I felt awful. Never before had I resigned. "My Cohen," I said, "I resign."

He laughed.

"You resign?"

What was so funny? Resign was serious business. "Yes. I resign."

"Resign?"

"Yes," I said.

"You?" he said. "You resign?"

"Yes," I said. "I resign."

"No you don't resign."

"Yes I do resign."

Then he explained.

"Presidents resign. Prime ministers resign. You?"

All this over a single word. Had I said something so terrible? Apparently yes. For Mr. Cohen was almost violently particular about this. That I was quitting...this bothered him not at all. That I was resigning...this infuriated him.

"You?" he said. "You quit."

He wanted me to say the words. I realized that by quitting, I was the weed picker that I was -- there among the worm, the ant, the rat. By resigning...by resigning I was soaring to the heights of presidents and prime ministers, and certainly well beyond the reach of Mr. Cohen.

No wonder he was outraged, especially when -- even after he offered to double my severance pay -- I still refused to quit.

No, I resigned.

10

The Purple Gang

My second job was with Mr. Roberts, a druggist on Park Avenue. I used to sweep the floors for him, but never good enough. He liked to say the boy before me had swept much better. I also ran deliveries for Mr. Roberts up and down Park Avenue. That wasn't so bad. Park Avenue was a boulevard. Bad were the side streets.

"Now I want you to go to one eleven Dubuc," Mr. Roberts said. "Okay?"

Mr. Roberts was a very clean man -- almost prissy. Whenever he looked at me, I felt filthy -- and stupid. Whenever he said something to me, there was a residue of wonderment in his eyes -- as though he could never be sure his words had penetrated my skull.

"Okay," I said.

47

"Dubuc Street," Mr. Roberts repeated, giving me an extra look.

"Okay."

"You're sure it's okay?"

"Sure it's okay."

"Well, all right then," he said. "One eleven."

Now why, I wondered, would he make such a deal over Dubuc? What was so special about Dubuc? Though I'd never walked the street, I knew it -- at least where it was -- near Mount Royal Mountain.

On my way I met Doodie. I told him where I was headed.

"You know who hangs out there on Dubuc?" he asked.

I did not know.

"The Purple Gang," he said...and from his expression, I assumed I was supposed to be startled.

But I had never heard of them before. They did sound awful, though. The Purple Gang.

"Well," I said, "I got to get going. I have a delivery to make."

Doodie wasn't finished.

"Did you hear what they did?"

Of course not.

"They shoved a guy down a sewer," Doodie said.

Now that sounded bad. The thought of it; shoving a guy down a sewer.

"That's news to me," I said.

Doodie said, "Where you been all your life?"

Doodie said things like that. He was the wisest and toughest guy on our street.

But even he feared The Purple Gang.

As for the guy they shoved down the sewer, surely they let him up again.

"Did they let him up again?" I said.

"No," Doodie said swiftly.

Doodie had made his point. But he added, "This delivery of yours, is it worth your life?"

For some reason, yes...yes it was.

* * *

Dubuc Street, when I got there, was empty, so far as people. But now I could hear voices from around the lampposts, and from between the bricks I saw eyes. The Purple Gang. They must be in hiding, I thought, preparing to snare me.

My delivery was at the end of the block and each step distanced me further from the safety of Park Avenue and took me deeper into -- who knew what?

I kept wondering what it must be like -- being stuffed down a manhole.

I even listened to the guy's voice, this guy they'd stuffed down.

Was he still alive? Hanging by his fingertips?

But I heard nothing.

Where were the people? Were they all so terrified of the Purple Gang that they never went outdoors?

I asked the lady who took the pharmacy package.

I said, "What about The Purple Gang?"

She slammed the door in my face.

Nice people here, I thought. They deserve a Purple Gang...though I saw no sign of them. I had imagined them all right, but then, perhaps so did everybody else. Maybe there was no Purple Gang except in the head...wouldn't that be something.

When I got back to the drugstore, Mr. Roberts gave me the stares. I had the feeling he had not expected me to return. He even seemed to check me limb for limb.

"Everything go okay?" he said.

"Yes," I said.

"Made the delivery all right?"

"Yes."

"Nothing happened?"

"No."

Now, Mr. Roberts was a man of reserve. But here he relented just a bit.

"The boy before you," he said, "he'd never go to Dubuc."

"Oh?"

"He was scared."

"Why?"

"Ever hear of The Purple Gang?"

"I guess so," I said.

I started back to get the broom. Mr. Roberts stopped me. He said, "Never mind. Forget that."

Escape from Mount Moriah

11

Nobody Knows Anything

When my father was old and far removed from his beginnings, he once told me, "Life is the process of learning who you are."

Back in Prochnik, Poland my father had been a prodigy, though in his day weren't they all? By the age of five he started Torah and at 10 he knew Torah and Mishnah. He mastered Gemara and Midrash by 15. The study of Hebrew Scripture knew no rest for himself and his generation.

Then he was drafted into the Czar's army and fought for the Czar in World War I. When he returned to Prochnik he found his home destroyed by soldiers of the same Czar. In the tradition of the Sages, his father had been wrapped in a Torah scroll, flesh and parchment set aflame. His sister had survived the pogrom and managed to flee to America. His mother had survived and she fled to Israel, which was then known as Palestine.

As for my father, he moved on to France, shaved his earlocks, married my mother, and went into business -- the leather trade. My mother had been the spoiled daughter of a French-Jewish aristocrat. She was a woman of taste. She was refined and delicate.

My father did all he could to keep up with her. He assimilated. But it never took. For a while, in France, he succeeded in business, and just when he was at his most successful, Hitler invaded.

I was born a month after the invasion, July 1940, and not until we settled in Montreal, some four years later, did I begin to know my father. He had lived a life. But it was a life out of sync.

Again in Montreal he turned to business. He had a talent for failure.

My mother used to say:

"Your father has no head for business."

So why did she prod him on?

Because she wanted the good things in life, the things that could not be bought on a scholar's income.

Left to his own choosing, the life of a scholar would have suited my father fine. He belonged in a House of Study, secluded from the turmoil of business, removed from the urgencies of daily cares. In a Yeshiva his knowledge of Torah could be stimulated, his wisdom put to the test -- and his worth as a scholar, and as a man, could be recognized and appreciated.

But that never happened.

He was a wanderer even among wanderers.

An indignation burned in him for all that was failed and missing in his life. How it angered him that a man who could not even quote a single passage of Torah could become a millionaire, and be seated in the front row of the synagogue, reaping respect and honors.

Where was the justice?

Such men were everywhere, ignoramuses. As for my father, he spent a life ascending the 49 levels of wisdom, and where was he? Where was he in terms of respect and honors?

At the bottom.

So he wandered from synagogue to synagogue trying to find his place, a place where men would call out his name and revere his interpretations of the divine laws and ordinances.

All of that is by way of saying that, as time when on, I was embarrassed to be with my father.

If all that I have said sounds self-pitying on the part of my father, then I have conveyed the truth. Except this. Is there a man who does not pity himself?

For me, the embarrassment began when a certain rabbi of a certain synagogue said, in his Sabbath sermon, that God had forbidden Israel to raise a king.

Now, my father excelled in pilpul, the minute details of Judaic scholarship -- but there was nothing pilpul about this. This was a clear and open error. "No, no, no," said my father, interrupting the solemn speech. In Yiddish, my father pointed out that, on the contrary, appointing a king is a steadfast law in Israel's 613 commandments. The Torah, he said, DEMANDS a king.

Of course, my father had broken into a man's speech, and that was rude. But he had not been reproachful. He had been polite, even timid, in his lecture -- and in his mind -- was only performing a traditional Yeshiva function -- that of engaging a fellow Talmudist in debate.

Did the congregation see it that way? Did the rabbi? Did the worshippers turn to my father with eyes of reverence as he cited chapter and verse? Not at all. They shook their heads and pounded their books in disapproval.

As for the rabbi, he ignored my father.

My father did not exist for him, and that was the great insult. All this knowledge and wisdom, what good did it do my father? Nobody listened. Nobody cared.

"Fools," my father told my mother. "Such fools."

So it was, Sabbath after Sabbath, synagogue after synagogue. Each time a rabbi was about to deliver a sermon, I'd get the jumps. I tried to excuse myself. I said to my father, "I'm going outside until it's over."

No. He insisted I stay, and sure enough the time came when the rabbi blundered and my father corrected him. By degrees my father grew bolder and bolder.

Later, at home, exasperated, he'd say, "Nobody knows anything."

And the reaction of the worshippers and the rabbis also increased in vehemence. People actually hissed when my father began to speak. Rabbis told him that if he had speeches to make, let him find his own congregation. It got so, that when my father arrived at a synagogue, any synagogue -- for his reputation had spread -- the gabbai would implore my father to remain silent for the sake of order.

My father would shrug, as if to say it was out of his hands. His silence depended on the accuracy of the rabbi. No. He, my father, was making no promises.

"Do you want order?" he asked. "Or truth?"

Usually, they wanted order.

As I grew up I stopped accompanying my father to the synagogue. But judging from his frustrations when he came home from services, nothing had changed.

What did he want? Nothing much. He wanted a man, even one man, who would slug it out with him pilpul by pilpul, intellect against intellect. All he wanted was one person, his equal, to hear him out from aleph to taph, and he never found him.

Then again, maybe there is no such person. For any of us.

12

A Sabbath Drive

Though my parents were thoroughly Jewish, they could never make up their minds about the practice of religion. Some days they were religious, some days they weren't. One Sabbath, it was all right to turn on the lights, the next Sabbath it was a sin.

To end the confusion, they decided to send me to a Yeshiva. They placed a yarmulke on my head and enrolled me in the Lubavitch Yeshiva on Montreal's Park Avenue.

Now the Lubavitch, as you may know, are very pious and thus, over a period of sustained training, I too became pious...quite the young fanatic. I even became a little tyrant in our home.

I began to quiz my father about why he worked on the Sabbath, why he didn't perform the mitzvah of tefillin every morning -- and what about the food? Was it kosher? I mean really kosher.

My parents, in time, were not Jewish enough for me. A choice was coming up. Either I leave the house and find parents worthy of my emerging Jewishness, or, they pull me out of the Yeshiva.

One thing I learned above all else in the Yeshiva -- you can't hide from sin. The Midrash says: "Know what is above you. An eye sees, an ear hears, and all your actions are recorded in a book."

One rabbi said, "In the time of reckoning even the walls will testify against you, and so will your angels and even your soul."

I believed this, but not enough. Without knowing it, I put it to the test -- just like King David who wrote, "Test me. Tempt me." And sure enough God sent him Bathsheba.

That summer we were up in the Laurentian Mountains spending the weekend in Val Moran with the Sterns, who owned a cottage in the woods.

On Friday I played with Lillia Stern. I told her Val Moran was nothing to me -- I was the toughest guy in town. That evening she repeated my movie line in the village square and that night twenty of the mean-est-looking characters were waiting for me at the bottom of the hill.

"Well?" said Lillia.

I went out to meet them and they fled. I don't know why. I was no match for even a single one of them, but by stepping out, who knew what they imagined?

The next day, the Sabbath, I decided to do without Lillia. Instead I found some green apples and tossed them into the open window of an empty red barn. When I got tired of that I went for a very long walk and found myself in a wilderness.

I was lost. The more I walked, the deeper was the isolation. Finally I found a road and waited for the first car. A French-Canadian farmer picked me up. He spoke no English. I spoke no French. So we were even. Somehow, he got me to where I belonged.

I made him let me off at the outskirts, so I'd not be seen riding on the Sabbath. I checked around. Nothing but woods. Do trees talk? Absolutely no eyes had seen me, no ears had heard me. There were no walls to testify against me. Surely the French-Canadian would be no witness. He knew nothing of me and to him this wasn't even the Sabbath.

Back in school a month or so later, the Rosh Yeshiva (headmaster) called me in and said he wanted to talk to me and my father. This was never a good sign -- when they wanted to talk to your father. The only thing I could figure was that he was behind on his payments, if he made any payments at all. Or, that I wasn't doing well enough in my studies. Maimonides I wasn't.

When I told my father about the summons, he shrugged. He said, "Nu, nu, nu."

Together, we stood before the rabbi, and this was what the rabbi said:

"Your son is being expelled. He was seen riding on the Sabbath."

"When was this?" asked my father.

The rabbi wouldn't say.

"Where was this?"

Same answer.

"Who saw him?" asked my father.

The rabbi smiled. But that was all.

Outside, my father asked me if it were true. I confessed. I told him about my Sabbath drive in Val Moran.

"You're sure nobody saw you?"

"I'm sure."

"Hmm..." he said.

13

A Telegram from Israel

One day a telegram came. I signed for it, since my parents were out, opened it, and read that my father's mother in Israel had died. "Gathered," said the message, "unto her people at age 102."

She had given birth to my father at a very late age, in the tradition of our matriarchs -- and what was she -- if not a matriarch? My father had spoken of her as of a saint.

I thought the news would be unbearable for my father, so I decided not to show him the telegram. I thought it best that he never know about his mother's death. What good would it do him to know?

I hesitate to call her my grandmother because I never met her and, as far as I knew, she never knew I existed. We were not a close family. My father seldom wrote to her, if ever.

But she was a legend, in the vein of Sarah, Rebecca, Leah and Rachel.

She had been a woman of Biblical beauty and virtue. There was a picture of her, seated on a bench, next to her husband, somewhere in the depths of Poland. He, long gray beard and lively eyes, had the appearance of a prophet, and she, yes, she was the image of a Jewish saint. She was truly a woman of another world, a world that existed no more.

I thought by withholding word of her death I would be preserving that world for my father. Enough of his past had collapsed. Why pain him even further?

So I kept it a secret for days and weeks and thought to go on like this forever. He'd never know, I thought. I was doing a great mitzvah, so nobly keeping the grief to myself.

Then, somewhere in my clothes, my mother found the telegram.

She asked, "What is this?"

She could not read English, so I told her. I told her everything, and as I explained my reasoning it occurred to me that I had done something terrible. I had performed no mitzvah. I had committed a sin.

I was overtaken by guilt and fear. This thing that I had done could not be undone. Upon such news, shiva had to be sat, kaddish had to be said, all at prescribed times. That time was lost.

For an instant I thought to enlist my mother in my conspiracy. But I dropped that scheme when I beheld her astonishment. I awaited the scolding, but nothing came.

That night I went out to visit a friend. On my way home the heavens opened, as though a celestial zipper had rent the sky. From utter darkness came incredible radiance. When I realized what was happening, it was over.

Wait, I thought. Wait. Wait. I want to see more. I want to see what's inside.

Somebody, it seemed, was showing me something, but I lacked the eyes to see. Was it a sign? This much I knew: It was not lightning. No, much too deliberate. What's more, this was not a flash, but rather a brilliance -- showing, or wanting to show, the answer to every secret.

My father had once said that when the world was created it was 56,000 times brighter than today. God had dimmed the world after the sin of Eve, our first matriarch, and would rekindle the original light when the earth, or perhaps an individual, was deserving.

When I got home my father was in his socks, in belated mourning for his mother. He had been weeping for her, but as for me and my sin, he was sympathetic. He said, "You silly child. You should have told me. But you meant well and what's done is done."

I told my father how the heavens had parted. That it had happened on the day he was praying for his mother's soul -- I said that must be coincidence.

He said there was no such thing.

14

A Sister from the Past

My father had a sister in Columbus, Ohio, and whenever he spoke of her he chuckled. Back a generation, when they had been children in Poland, they had been at odds in usual brother and sister fashion -- or perhaps more than usual.

Dinah, as my father told it, had a special fondness for flowers. She spent the better part of her days attending row after row of flower pots, which were artfully arranged around the four walls of her bedroom -- some even hanging from the ceiling.

In hasty revenge for a spat between them, my father broke into her room and systematically smashed every single flower pot. They were very young then, my father and his sister, but from that point on relations between them were difficult, as you'd expect -- especially from her side.

Of course, from that time in the early 1900s to the early 1950s, the world had flip-flopped once and twice. The family had been scattered and there were deaths, marriages, births -- and for those who survived -- aging. Dinah was about 10 years older than my father, which put her near 60.

"She must be an old woman now," my father would say. Then he'd chuckle. Still...the memory of the smashing of the flower pots...as though nothing else had ever happened between them.

I asked my father why, after all this time, he made no attempt to get together with his sister. All these years apart -- they were brother and sister after all! Wasn't he curious?

Not really, but he did write to her anyway and she returned a 20-page letter filled on both sides with an outpouring of sibling lovesickness. She was a widow (she wrote), had raised four boys and now...now she was alone. Could she come visit?

A year later my father wrote back, saying yes.

We met her at the train station and an old woman she was all right. How would he greet her, I wondered, given the span of time between them? Sure enough, there were no hugs, no kisses -- only a nod from the two of them -- none of the emotions you usually see from others at times like these.

I thought -- did she also remember the flower pots? Or was it just the way things were in our family.

My father, as I've already said, lived by King Solomon's dictum, "This too shall pass." The entire family, then, lived by this code that made them so terse and unloving, at least on the surface.

Judging from the amount of baggage, Dinah was not visiting. She was prepared to move in with us -- and we lived in a single room. There she stayed with us and grew more disenchanted each day.

Throughout that time there was absolutely nothing between my father and his sister -- no reminiscing, no shared memories, nothing -- nothing to show them as relatives, as friends, or even as strangers. As for me, Dinah kept aloof except for her questions.

What astonished her was our poverty.

She hadn't the courage to ask my father directly (what would he smash now?), so she asked me.

When she'd find me alone, she'd say, "Why no money? Why are you so poor?"

As if it were my fault. Or as if it were my father's fault.

I had no answers for her questions.

In fact, is there an answer for such a question -- why are you poor? I mean, what can you say except that I am poor because I have no money. I have no money because I am poor. To defend my father I once said, "He works very hard."

She said, "Yes, but..."

Financially, she'd done well in America. To her mind, if you worked hard you made money. How sensible. Except that life was not sensible. Because of her thinking, she even suspected that my father did make money, but squandered it away.

"What," she asked me, "does he do with the money?"

That, I could not answer, either.

I told my father about her questions and he too was stumped, not to mention embarrassed, humbled, and humiliated. Yet he never reproved her for the discord she was planting in our home.

But I did have hard feelings against her.

She used to call me "Yakki." This instead of Jack or Jackie or Yaacov or Yankle. More than anything, even more than her questions, that is what made me dislike her. I thought, if only she would stop calling me Yakki.

Why didn't I ask her to stop? Because even at this young age I was amazed how nothing works out. This was just another one of those things. Anyway, this too shall pass.

Finally, I said to my father, "She calls me Yakki, you know."

"Nu?" he said.

"I don't like the name."

"I'll talk to her," he said.

The next day she did not call me Yakki. She drew me near to her, tears in her eyes, hugged me, kissed me, and kept repeating, "Yaacov, Yaacov, Yaacov."

A day later she was packed and gone.

15

The Fairmount Synagogue Choir

The Fairmount Synagogue choir was something wonderful. The synagogue was famous for its grand architecture and its cantor, who had an international reputation. But the choir -- a sweet collection of young voices -- made it special above all else.

People came from everywhere to hear this choir, which was led by the temperamental and even violent Israel Korbik. Mr. Korbik terrorized the choir boys -- and this was no small thing. These were Jewish toughs from Esplanade, St. Urbain, Jeanne Mance. Even after a Sabbath performance, decked out in the splendor of white tunics, chanting such praises as Holy, Holy, Holy, nothing holy transpired in the alley back of the synagogue, where fights broke out between us just for the sake of a fight.

My mother used to say, "I send you to shul just to come home with a bloody nose?"

There was one untouchable among us. This was Ronnie Stone. He was our peer, but only in age. In virtually every other way, he was superior. He was our soloist and had so clear and fine a voice that it was said to ascend through all 13 heavenly gates of prayer.

Even Mr. Korbik was in awe of him. The way he talked to the rest of us, harshly and impatiently, was not the way he talked to Ronnie. The way he punched, pinched, smacked, and booted the rest of us -- well, certainly that was not his way with Ronnie.

Unlike the usual seating arrangements, where the best students begin from the right and left of the master, we saw to it that the newest and worst member was seated nearest to Mr. Korbik, to be ready and accessible for Mr. Korbik's blows.

As for me, I was always -- it seemed -- the newest and the worst. As Ronnie was one extreme, I was the other. I had no voice. I did not even have an ear.

I was surprised to hear this.

My father had once visited Mr. Korbik to find out how I was doing.

"He says you have no ear," my father reported. I took it literally.

Mr. Korbik liked to hit me. The Sabbath, our day of holy rest, became for me a day of dreaded conflict.

On the Sabbath I was beaten publicly, before the entire congregation. This was unjust because the sour notes Mr. Korbik was hearing came not from me. Usually I mouthed the words. I mean, I faked the singing, except for "Amen," at which I was very good.

Thus I was the scapegoat -- and perhaps for that reason -- I was important to the other choir boys.

Now, for Sabbath and festivals, we performed in the center of the sanctuary, assembled in a semicircle on a platform. There were special occasions, however, when we were above, on the upper tier, hidden from view in the women's section. That was the case on Sundays, when we sang at weddings.

On Sundays, by the way, Mr. Korbik paid us for the week. He paid us what he thought we were worth and sometimes I got nothing, which goes to show how unfair it is when you are paid on merit.

Once, in December, two very rich and influential families were being united in marriage. I knew this because all of us were to be there that Sunday when, for most weddings, only the best were selected. Ronnie, of course, was the main attraction. He sang "Because."

But for this wedding, I was included and I asked Mr. Korbik where we'd be singing -- down in public or up out of view? "Why do you want to know?" asked Mr. Korbik, his eyes blazing and his fists coiled to strike. What had I asked that was so dangerous?

Nothing. Except that Mr. Korbik hated everything about me.

"Upstairs," Mr. Korbik finally said, but not to me. I heard him tell Ronnie and was privileged to overhear. Overhearing was how I was spoken to in the choir room. I was not important enough to be told anything directly and Ronnie, of course, never talked to me since I was mortal.

Upstairs. That meant I could wear whatever I wanted, even stay in my boots, since nobody would see us, and, as it happened, it did snow that Sunday, and though we all changed into our white tunics, I kept my boots on -- dripping mud and snow. But so what? We would be going upstairs, using a back stairway.

For a moment, instinct told me to remove my boots, in case of a change of plans. But I kept my boots on, even though I was some contrast, white linen covering my body, boots covering my feet.

My instinct had been right.

As we filed out from the choir room, Mr. Korbik said, "They want us downstairs."

There was no time to remove my boots and with these terrible boots I stormed through the carpeted aisles of the sanctuary. My boots spoiled the mood of the whole business. The wedding guests pointed. Some laughed, some gasped.

Mr. Korbik gradually became aware of the commotion, but not the cause. Who could it be except me? He glanced me up and down, beheld my boots, and in his face I saw murder.

Right after this he fired me. He said, "You're fired. Don't come back."

I took the hint and returned only now and then as a Sabbath worshipper.

From afar, once again the choir was so beautiful.

16

We Go Borrowing

Borrowing money can become a habit and it became a habit that trapped my parents, who were always short on money and long on dreams. They borrowed from friends -- people who owed them favors stemming from Europe. This was not my parents at their best, and people did judge them -- including me. But survival can be an ugly business and who can say what is right and what is wrong?

Sometimes my parents brought me along when they went borrowing -- and it was always unpleasant. I knew the spiel, how they had suffered under the Nazis and wanted nothing now but to get back on their feet. My mother cried at all the right places and it was all true and sincere and at the same time very uncomfortable. They lost their friends through this, one by one.

As for Mr. Wernstock, he was an exceedingly wealthy man, but it had not always been so. In

Europe he had worked for my father as a cutter. My father had owned a handbag factory in Toulouse and then the Nazis marched in and took it over only months before we made the escape from France to Spain to Portugal and finally to Montreal. We had all arrived on the same boat, the Serpa Pinto, a Portuguese pineapple freighter in which we, the remnants of a generation, made our voyage from the old world to the new. Mr. Wernstock had landed on his feet, swiftly converting his savings into a fortune and leaving my father very far behind.

One Friday night we took the streetcar up to Outremont, the prettiest section, where Mr. Wernstock lived in a castle, surrounded by lawns and fences and stables and tennis courts.

My father was very nervous. He had not been invited and was using chutzpah instead. He had been trying to reach Mr. Wernstock by phone but could not get him in the office. Mr. Wernstock's office was on St. Catherine Street, on the 22nd floor of the Wernstock Building.

Observing this fantasyland that was Outremont, my father said, "He was nothing but a cutter for me, you know." In case Mr. Wernstock forgot, my father would remind him -- humorously, of course.

"Many times," my father said, "I lent him money." This was hard for me to believe, but I knew it to be true. There was talk that Mr. Wernstock was person-ally worth 50 million dollars. My father was asking for but five thousand of that -- pocket money -- the kind of money Mr. Wernstock used for change.

"Do you remember Mr. Wernstock?" my father asked. I said I did not.

"Ha," my father said. "He used to bounce you on his lap."

My mother was staying home for this trip. This was between the men, two industrialists head to head. Big business deals were to be discussed. My father had said more than just money was in the offing. Maybe even a partnership. Maybe Mr. Wernstock would bring him into the business.

My father had assured my mother that certainly he'd not go in as a common employee, or even a common executive. No, something like a partnership would have to be arranged. Already my father could see himself as "Mr. Inside," running all of Mr. Wernstock's factories. Of course, if worse came to worse, $5,000 would do.

My father now rang the bell by the entrance gate. A voice asked his name. A servant came to unlock the gate. My father said, "You stay here. I may be a while."

I was prepared to wait hours. Not in ten minutes do two men discuss partnerships. But within that time, ten minutes, my father was back, his eyes fixed on something painful in the distance. He said nothing, nothing to me, nothing later to my mother, and never again was Mr. Wernstock's name mentioned. He had

said something dreadful to my father, and I never
knew what it was.

17

A Jewish Soldier

My father loved Israel, the ancient and the modern. He also loved America and there was no question of divided loyalty because America and Israel were one and the same.

"If you love Israel," he said, "you love America."

"If you love America, you love Israel."

America was the embodiment of the Jewish dream.

"And what is the Jewish dream?" said my father. "Listen to the words of Micah our prophet: 'And each man shall sit under his vine and fig tree, and none shall make him afraid.'"

Said my father: "What is that, if not the Jewish dream? And what is that if not the American dream!"

* * *

My father wept the day Israel was declared a state. I was eight years old then and we had already been three years in Montreal. I was too young to understand everything about Israel, but on the event of its rebirth, I knew something extraordinary was happening.

Daily that spring the Yiddish newspaper from New York documented the events of the Arab-Jewish conflict. Each morning my father walked along Fairmount Street to Abe's News Store to bring back *Der Tag*. For a man who knew pogroms in Poland, where Jews lived from fright to fright, the tales of daring Jews astonished him -- Jews who hearkened back to the days of Joshua and David.

One day I went out to meet my father as he returned with the paper.

"Look," he said, pointing to a photo on the front page. "A Jewish soldier."

Then I saw him crying and understood how incredible this was.

Now during this time we were menaced regularly by the French gangs that marched up from below St. Lawrence Street -- the dividing line between French and English-speaking Montreal.

We were tough ourselves -- meaning Doodie and Benjie and Yehudie and all the rest -- but we were no match for these French -- Pepsis we called them -- who had the advantage of genetic indignation. They were passionately resentful against anything "English" and anything that wasn't French was English.

Also, they surpassed us in numbers -- there seemed no end to them. Down below St. Lawrence they were bred for hatred, raised for thuggery. Up from St. Lawrence, they came in waves and attacked. Their crazed ferocious violence needed no provocation -- only bodies, and here we were. Especially Sundays.

Then they'd be waiting for us at the Talmud Torah Hebrew School. In the province of Quebec, children under 13 were not allowed in regular movie houses. There had once been a theater fire, kids trampled to death, causing such a law to be passed. Schools, however, were exempt, so on Sunday afternoons we flocked to the Talmud Torah for Laurel and Hardy, Roy Rogers and Gene Autry.

I do not use the word "flocked" in vain -- because sheep that we were, we fell to the blows of the Pepsis who were gathered by the entrance of the Talmud Torah and punished us coming and going.

Fight back? Who ever heard of the words?

But that week, Israel had been declared a state, and that Sunday there had been a photo of a Jewish soldier -- and everything changed. We let them have their way when we entered the Talmud Torah, but once inside the darkened auditorium there was no longer that sense of terror. Something unspoken passed between us. We were of a single mind.

After the movies, which nobody really watched, the lights came on and we rushed for the doors. I was somewhere in the middle of this army and by the time I got out the fighting had already begun.

Doodie was pummeling the leader of the Pepsis, a boy twice his size. Doodie had him propped against a car, striking him repeatedly in the midsection. The Pepsi grew weak in the knees and wobbled to the pavement.

This gave us the courage and we went after them one by one. As for the Pepsis -- first they were stupefied. What was this? Jews fighting back? Next, they turned and tried to run, but we caught them and gave measure for measure. We repaid all debts and even made some deposits for the future.

When I got home, I was covered in blood. My mother made me take a bath. She kept muttering about this and that and, as for my father, he gave me a wink and a big secret smile.

18

The Old Men in the Synagogue

The old men in the synagogue have always been there for me. They were there again this year. Each year at this time I worry that they will all be gone, dead from old age, taking with them the "flame."

Of course, some day they will all be gone, and I wonder who will take their place. Certainly not my generation. We were raised, as the rabbi says, to be polite "excuse me" Jews.

As for the old men, they came from the outlands of Russia and Poland, and there was nothing varnished about them. They brought with them a singular heritage, and they knew nothing else but to be emphatically Jewish.

To me, they are a comfort. They make me eternal.

In these Days of Awe, I make my yearly visit to the small Orthodox synagogue, and I am a stranger. I hate myself for all that I do not know. I can't read the Hebrew (not as well as they can) and I don't know when to sit or rise or say "Amen." I just follow what the old men do.

The old men know everything.

The synagogue is their home. They feel obliged to welcome strangers. They hand me the prayer book and, every so often, point me to the right page. "We are now saying the SHEMA," says an old man.

"Hear, O Israel, the Lord is our God, the lord is One."

They sit by their own table and devout as they are, they sometimes gossip amid the prayers. Gossip to them is what Abraham said to Sarah. They also discuss the news -- the Deliverance from Egypt.

The past is more real to them than the present.

"You should wear warmer clothes," an old man says to me. "In Auschwitz, it got cold early. The people who brought light clothes, they had no chance. Always wear warm clothes. I know what I'm talking about."

Many of them go back before Auschwitz, back to the upheavals of the 1920s. Each endured a different hardship, escaped a different tyrant -- but they all studied, and learned practically by heart the Five Books of Moses.

The cantor now chants the ancient melodies, refrains that have endured from exile to exile.

"He is excellent today," says an old man, speaking of the cantor. "He knows what he is saying. Notice how he squeezes all the right words. Excellent."

"Why," I ask, "is it so important to squeeze the right words?"

"Why?" says the old man. "I'll tell you why. When you go before a judge, you demand the best lawyer to plead your case. Today we are before the highest judge. The cantor is our lawyer."

Yes, these are the Days of Judgment.

On the first day of the year -- goes the prayer -- it is inscribed, and on the Fast Day of Atonement, it is sealed and determined, how many shall pass by, and how many shall be born; who shall live and who shall die, who shall finish his allotted time, and who not.

The rabbi -- a man from old Russia who speaks passionately of his love for America -- sits in a corner to the left of the Holy Ark, wrapped in his prayer shawl, the picture of an ancient prophet. All of his grown sons are rabbis.

Next to him stands his youngest, an 11-year-old son who apes his father in words and gestures.

"You shall love the Lord with all your heart, with all your soul, and with all your might. And these words which I command you today shall be upon your heart. You shall teach them thoroughly to your children."

During the reading of the Torah, the boy is in the hallway, perfecting his Julius Erving jump shot.

* * *

Not much has changed.

In my youth, the Days of Awe meant Rosh Hashanah and Yom Kippur and the World Series. And one year, the Los Angeles Dodgers' great pitcher, Sandy Koufax, would not pitch on Yom Kippur. That was a source of pride to Jews, especially to those who were Yankees fans.

And today, I would still rather be asked Ted Williams' lifetime batting average than be asked up to read the Torah...I have the answer for Williams.

The rabbi's sermon is on that very subject. He is worried about "the golden chain of our heritage" that is about to be broken.

As he spoke those words nearly 20 years ago, it had occurred to me then, that I was now 42 -- and when my father was that age, he was an old man -- one of the "old men in the synagogue."

He also knew everything.

Years from now, I wonder, who will be there to show me the right page, and will there be any old men left for my son? He is only 2 years old, and the old men cover him with love.

To them, he is the flame. He is their eternity.

Introduction

It Continues with Tevee Skulnick

Now it's many years later and all of us or most of us are in the United States, married with children and even grandchildren. Here comes an e-mail from Tevee Skulnick and this, a voice from the past, is so pleasant. We lost touch in Montreal soon after Fairmount School though I saw him a few times later when he became an active Zionist and spoke perfect Hebrew and later went to Israel. He fought.

Now he was back, married and living in Florida. Boca Raton, I think though not sure. But it was Florida. So here's the e-mail and he asks if I am the same broken-toothed kid who is now famous for writing the novel *Indecent Proposal*. He saw the movie and read the book and is not surprised. There was always something of the dreamer about me.

The two of us were different from the rest, the rest of the kids at Fairmount School, which he said was torn down and no longer exists, and what a shame! (Or maybe not.) But we were daffy, each of us, and that is why we became friends and usually walked together and fought together inside the schoolyard and out. We were different together.

We even had our own language. No one else understood this language because only we knew the truth, that life was absurd and not to be taken seriously. We joked and laughed, between ourselves, at all forms of pomposity. We saw through it all, and this too got us in trouble.

Some learn this early and some learn this late, that at times only by spoofing hypocrisy can we endure the hypocrisy that surrounds us.

Tevee got expelled a few times. The pointed finger so often seemed to land on him. But he was a good kid, loyal.

If I got into a scrap, I could always count on Tevee, who never backed down for himself or for a friend.

Montreal was a tough town and no matter how old you were there was someone out to get you for no reason.

If you were yellow you were yellow forever, so you had to fight.

Frequently in the schoolyard, at recess, the boys split between the Roy Rogers Gang and the Gene Autry Gang. We attacked in waves. The fistfights were pretend and so were the gunshots, but you were always marked as belonging to one gang or another, and quickly you learned that in life you would have to choose sides. There was no middle and there was no giving up and Tevee never gave up.

In our after-class Hebrew school, Montreal's Talmud Torah, this is where we were further intro-duced to the Torah as the Word of God transmitted through Moses...and as the road leading to Zionism. The devotion and passion for Zion never left either one of us, not then, not ever. We pretty much picked up where we left off.

So now all these years later we agreed to stay in touch. We began corresponding by phone, in addition to the e-mails, and if my story was not as glamorous as people thought it was – I was supposed to be rich and living the life of a Famous Author! – his story was quite sad. He was very sick, a very sick old man. Tevee? The loopy kid with the wild streak and the untamed hair – old? Yes, Tevee.

He worked odd jobs in the synagogue and what he did up to that time, in Montreal, in Israel, in the United States, was too long to tell.

He may have told it to me, but it escapes me now, maybe because none of it is cheerful. I had hoped for better news from someone who had been such a dear friend back in the 1940s and part of the 1950s. We reminisced about that, about how we made fun of the teachers and how the principal, Mr. Webster, scared the heebie-jeebies out of us. When we were rowdy in the schoolyard during recess, all he had to do was step out and glare at us through those glasses, and that was enough.

Tevee was usually there, in the principal's office. He was always doing something, something wrong.

"There was no name for it at the time," Tevee explained, "but I had ADD, Attention Deficit Disorder."

Tevee, as I may have said earlier, was part of a big family, and a wonderful family. He had four older brothers, all big and tough (as was the father) and they were in the furniture moving business. They were all big and tough but they were so very sweet and reverential around their mother. They would do nothing to displease her. She ruled the home, as is usual among Jewish families, starting, perhaps, with our Biblical Sarah. (In a dispute between husband and wife, God told Abraham, "Listen to your wife"...and so it has been ever since.)

The brothers were equally kind-hearted towards one another and of course to their father, but let no outsider try any business.

This was not a religious home but it was a Jewish home and this is where some of the trouble began.

"You were always in the principal's office," I reminded Tevee as we laughed about our past, as if it were the good old days.

(I have fought in wars and been with generals, prime ministers, presidents and even a king, but still today nothing sends shivers like *the principal wants you in his office.*)

"They didn't know what it was," Tevee said. "If they had known, maybe it would have been different."

These days he was barely making a living. He was taking all kinds of medicines for his various ailments. He wanted me to move my family next to him in Florida.

Of course that was impossible.

"I'm so glad you succeeded," he said, as if to say that he had failed. I explained that I had not succeeded and that he had not failed. Struggles were still ahead. Plenty. Our troubles may be different but they are troubles just the same. This knowledge like-wise comes with wisdom or with age, that no man can accuse his neighbor of being lucky. We don't know.

Onto the question of success and failure, I could seldom find the difference between the two. Was my father a failure? In business, yes. But he saved his family. He had that one moment of heroism and to my mind this triumphs over his years of futility and tops him over and above Bill Gates.

Luck, though – luck is everything. I have said this elsewhere often enough and it is still true. Luck can't be bought.

Some people anguish and work hard all their lives but fail. They should not be judged. Neither should people who have succeeded. They too have secrets.

Never ask a stranger too many questions. You're better off not knowing.

But it wasn't all bad from Tevee. We usually ended up laughing from one phone call to another.

He had begun reading the 18 stories from this memoir. He phoned to say that he enjoyed them very much, only he longed for more.

And why wasn't he being mentioned!

So now he is.

But it will never be enough. There is so much more say. But do we still have the time? Do we still have the skills?

Does anybody care?

* * *

Tevee is gone. One day a promised phone call never came. So I phoned and was given the news.

At some point in life things move faster than you would like.

Youth recaptured is difficult but, to keep my promise to Tevee and to others who have asked for more, I have gone ahead and written more.

Please do not expect sequence. Stay with me as I let it go as it comes. Life is like that, disorderly, so writing should be the same, if it is to be honest.

Linear is too tidy and life is not tidy. Remember what Rashi said (relative to Scriptures): There is no before or after.

If events appear out of place here, well then, I was only following my instincts at the writing and as every writer, or horseplayer knows – trust your first instinct because there is no second instinct. You only get one chance to be true to your subconscious, which is where true writing begins.

Along the following pages we go back, further, into the ordinary and extraordinary days and nights of a refugee kid opening his eyes to a new world.

Along the writing I was tempted to stop and check for facts, but are facts more reliable than impressions? I vote for impressions.

Facts give you time and place, but impressions give it how it really was. Marcel Proust did it without Google.

I say let it tumble, let it ride...it's all a toss of the dice anyway.

But this is not a story for kids. Yes it is, but it is also (perhaps mostly) for grown-ups.

Keep in mind that as a kid, I never suffered. There were no concentration camps for me or my family. We escaped from Toulouse, France just in time.

Long story.

Hard times, yes, but I never suffered.

I was born July 20, 1940. Hitler arrived in France a month earlier – so you can imagine.

The stories here take place at the outset of our arrival in Montreal in 1944, the second day of Passover.

How this took place after we were turned back from Philadelphia by FDR is another long story. It took my father, Noah, 10 long years to get the right papers to finally settle us in the United States. For me, this began in Cincinnati, that most American of all American towns, at least back then. This had been Ozzie and Harriet territory.

But mostly here it is about Montreal. What years? I'd say about 1945 until about 1955, which would make me aged five to 15. Maybe 16 or even older.

Depends on this and that, wherever my memory takes me.

Why that period? Well I am not historic but the times were. There had been a Holocaust.

Oops. Almost forgot. Tevee had reminded me where I had lived in Montreal (at least for a time), and that was 5050 St. Urbain.

Directly across the street as I was growing up a kid 10 years older was already quite grown and destined to become Canada's greatest writer and literary figure.

Mordecai Richler.

I did not know this of course, at the time.

There are many things I did not know, but here are some things I do know.

19

My Three Heroes

King David tops my list of people I admire. I have my reasons, most of them to be found in his Book of Psalms, which contains the greatest writing of all time. He was a warrior, a king, but also a poet, and also so humble. He is the father of prayer, the master of forgiveness. He sinned, with Bathsheba. So great as he was, he was not perfect. He says so in his Psalms. He keeps asking God to spare him from being put to shame (against his enemies). Who can't identify with that?

From childhood onward, he was hounded by troubles, and this too we can understand. We all have troubles, and King David describes them for us.

He wrote all that 3,000 years ago in Jerusalem. Every thought still dazzles. Every word still glows.

Throughout his travails, his faith never dimmed. If only I could find such durable fidelity. I try.

Amalek (anti-Semitism in its various forms) is still everywhere, even re-ignited. This is where the 20th Century began.

Now in the 21st Century our kids and grandkids must face this all over again. Can a merciful God really let this happen?

King David would have the answer. I don't.

It started when I found myself (now in Montreal) being introduced to a new classroom of kids. A particular Jewish holiday was being celebrated.

"Here," said the teacher, "you will be King David."

She placed a (plastic) silver crown over my brow. I hardly knew what she was talking about; English still new to me. But I was anointed.

From then onward there was no power to take that crown off my head.

My second all-time hero is Beethoven. Sarah, my sister, loved classical music, hence Beethoven, of course, and so it followed with me.

Beethoven is like King David, ever reaching upwards to touch the heavenly throne of glory. I still insist that King David's Psalms inspired Beethoven.

Here's a twist, and not a good one. My agent said that Paramount Pictures had found a screenwriter to turn my novel *Indecent Proposal* into film. They had settled on Amy Holden Jones. The novelist seldom does the screenwriting, this too I have observed, and without complaints from me. I was onto my next novel, besides.

So I looked her up, this Jones, and initially found that she had written a movie (later many sequels) about Beethoven.

How perfect!

But in Hollywood, as in life, nothing is perfect. This is also true.

Searching further, I saw that this Beethoven of hers was...was a dog. She had named a dog Beethoven. How cheap is that!

That was like the novelist who used Kafka in the title, but this Kafka was also a dog, or something.

I hate cheap tricks like this.

I am sure that an entire generation has grown up thinking that Beethoven is the name of a dog.

This is quite outrageous, and speaking of forgiveness, I can never forgive Miss Jones for such deception.

Beethoven, the real Beethoven, composed the most sublime music known to civilization. No one competes, no one compares.

This much is strange. You never hear a Beethoven symphony for the first time. Even if technically you do hear it for the first time, somehow it sounds familiar.

There is something mystical about this.

One thing about a Beethoven sonata or symphony, you cannot do something else at the same time, like writing, texting or vacuuming.

You must not do this.

That would be sacrilege.

This is not elevator music or dental music.

For Beethoven everything must stop.

Anything from Beethoven is a religious experience.

Beethoven took Mozart a step further, but no one took Beethoven a step further.

Next comes Maurice "Rocket" Richard. He was King David and Beethoven on ice. He was a ball of fire. He was the greatest hockey player of all time.

I give you Bobby Orr and Gordie Howe, but when Richard jumped over the boards, touched the puck and zoomed toward the net, the world held its breath in anticipation and amazement. The Forum roared. His eyes – those blazing eyes! – were fixed upon the purity of scoring goals. He was insatiable. He won eight Stanley Cups for the Canadiens.

He was the first to score 50 goals in a 50 game season. He retired as the leading goal scorer of all time. He contributed more goals than assists which says something about his rage, his rage to win. He skated as if being pursued by something other than the other team. Asked how come he scored so many goals, the response was simple: "I shoot da puck."

Statistics do no justice to Richard. You had to be there!

But it is off the ice where I grew to admire Richard. There was no swagger to him. He was humble. He was in mid-career when the Separatist troubles began. But no politics for him. He was about the game and only the game and only scoring goals and only winning and that was it and that was all.

Once, I think, he took a stand; some letter to the editor about French hockey players being treated unfairly by "English" owners.

But otherwise he let the game do his talking.

I submit that everyone is a genius at something. The trick is to find out what it is. Not everyone is so fortunate. Richard found his genius in the game of hockey.

For King David and for Beethoven the blessing of genius could not have been timelier or more perfect.

So why would I bring up Moses at such a time? Because for all his justifiable claims to fame, Moses was recognized by the Torah itself for his most powerful attribute...

Humility.

Maybe this, humility, is what binds my three heroes beyond all other skills.

20

So This Is Life

We had already been in Montreal a few years but moved around so much, house to house, room to room, the four of us, that I was always the new kid. Time after time I was the new kid on the block, the new kid in school, the new kid in class. I had to make new friends and new enemies all over again.

Is it any wonder that I flunked 3rd Grade?

That is not supposed to happen.

Nobody flunks 3rd Grade.

The excuse was that moving around so much never gave me time to do homework. Or living in rooms as we did (sometimes) never gave me a place to study.

Or that I had just given up, at age eight, nine or 10, or 11, figuring that formal education would never work out for me.

I would have to do it on my own.

In some of the homes where we moved to there were books, and I devoured them all. I especially liked Sherlock Holmes.

In one place – on Esplanade? – they had *Encyclopedia Britannica*, one volume about 2,000 pages.

Between baseball and hockey, down on the lane, where I scored winning goals and tape-measure homeruns, I decided to read it from A to Z.

Don't know how far I got, but pretty far.

How I got from Grade 3 (a second time) to Grade 4, 5, 6, and 7, this is a mystery. It is murky, I mean how I passed any test. How I got into high school (several yeshivas and Baron Byng) and out of high school, this too is a mystery. Same for college – who, what, where, when, why?

Or maybe it's that I still could not speak the language too well, English. (I was born speaking French but arrived speaking Spanish. Long story.)

But we were talking about the 3rd Grade the first time in Fairmount School. We had moved again so I was the new kid again. What a frightening building, this school. It was like an angry person. The windows were lit up like eyes. It was all bricks and chains and fences and it took up a whole block.

I had a note to present to the teacher, Miss Walters. I was late and I was scared. The door was open and there were about 30 kids in there, half of them girls in pigtails or ponytails sitting proper, so pretty. The boys looked tough. (I knew that I would have to get tough myself, and quick.) Miss Walters also had a note about me.

She hushed the class. She told them that I was special. That I had just arrived from France and the war that they had been studying – "and look at those eyes! Isn't he a handsome young boy? What a darling young addition to our class." Then, "We are so glad to have you with us, Jacques, safe and sound in Montreal."

I blushed throughout all that and was embarrassed but also very glad to be given so much love. The girls smiled and giggled. The boys still looked tough.

"Make yourself welcome," said Miss Walters, smiling. "Have a seat."

So this is life, I thought. Not bad. Not bad at all.

Next day I was late again and stood by the door waiting for Miss Walters to start it all over again, the gushing.

"Well?" she said, staring me down. "What are you waiting for? Do you need a formal invitation? Take your seat and behave."

So this is life.

Escape from Mount Moriah

21

I Live Barbara

I guess this is what you call your first crush and it was Barbara and I fell for her right from the start, there in Fairmount School, Grade 3, or 4 or 5, or all of them together. She sat a distance from me in class, somewhere up front, near the teacher. She was dark-haired and ivory-skinned. Those eyes! There was something different about her, besides being the most beautiful girl around. There was a seriousness about her that set her apart.

There is always someone with whom you wish to share your secrets and for me, this was Barbara. I knew she would understand.

There was much to tell.

I was in love with Barbara. I loved Barbara. I even loved the name. Barbara.

In the morning at Fairmount School, first thing was standing at attention and singing God Save the Queen – or was it still the king?

In any case, that's why the French attended schools and lived in neighborhoods separate from us.

As the other girls took that moment to check around the room for cute boys, Barbara never did. Barbara never had to do anything so cheap.

I think she noticed me. Well she had to. We shared the same classroom. We shared it for Reading. This gave me trouble. The English language was still new to me. I was born in France, as noted, and we escaped to Spain, as noted. There in Franco's Spain we spent about two years in hiding. This was in Barcelona where we lived with false papers.

My father, Noah, and mother, Ida, were so fretful of my being whisked away from where we lived in secret that they drummed into me the address (which is with me to this day); Calle Valencia doscientos treinta y seis – which is, Calle Valencia 236. They made me repeat it a thousand times.

Of all the addresses of mine, this one I will never forget.

From Spain we set off to Portugal to board the Serpa Pinto, which would take us to the New World. This was a lucky ship. Others were sunk by German U-Boats.

Long story.

So when we arrived in Montreal, when I was four years old, I spoke some French, some Spanish, some Yiddish and was only beginning to learn English, thanks to the radio and thanks to my sister Sarah who was eight years older. (So she actually saw Germans directing traffic in French Toulouse. In her memoir, when my name comes up, I find myself, a toddler, sleeping through the Holocaust.) Between the two of us, we only spoke English here in Montreal.

She caught on to the language fast and I idolized and idealized my sister Sarah...but in school and in my dreams there was Barbara.

I wondered if she ever noticed me as apart from the others. I tried not to stare. I became jealous when another boy started talking to her.

I once saw her laughing when Arnold told her a joke and I was crushed and hated Arnold evermore. I was funnier than he was. Just give me a chance.

Just give me a chance, Barbara.

I was shy and I stuttered, sometimes, and would she laugh at me for my French accent?

I stuttered, it was said, because up in the Pyrenees, during the escape and in hiding from the Gestapo, my mouth was filled with cotton to keep me from bawling or from making any sound. The fright of this may have caused the problem that came in childhood later on. Or maybe it's because I was allegedly born left-handed and my parents trained me to be strong from the right side.

I never told anyone about my love for Barbara except for Tevee.

"I loveth Barbara," I told Tevee.

"Does she knowith thee?"

"I doth not knowith."

"I wish thee goodeth luckith."

We spoke like that sometimes when we could not wear off the ritual of our morning hymns and a few times we were caught doing this in class.

I may have told my mother about Barbara and if I did, she must have smiled. She had other problems.

Since I was a terrible student and had already given up on school, I dreamed of Barbara, even in class and throughout class.

If only I could do something heroic to catch her. Something came up. The biggest kid in class, Felmore, had it in for me from the start. He was a bully all around but for me he had it special. That day he turned around and gave me the fight sign, which was a high fist pump. Everyone saw this, the boys and the girls and that meant Barbara, if only she cared.

He passed around a note that everyone saw and when it got to me it read, "After school."

I wrote back, "Okay," and the note was passed to him.

I was in for a fight. There was no choice.

Now all day through class I dreamed about the fight and I knew that, win or lose, I had to show up.

Which I did. So did the rest of the class. Some of the boys had been betting that I would never show up.

For some reason, when the time came, I wasn't scared.

Maybe I learned that from my father. When the time came in Toulouse, he knew what he had to do.

So there I was, in the schoolyard, but Felmore – it was Felmore who chickened out. There was no sign of him.

The next day in class the boys looked at me differently and Barbara turned and gave me a smile.

But that wasn't enough. Nothing else happened. I wanted it like in the movies, where they kiss.

That day the teacher gave out the English Reader for a special chapter about something and when the book came to me I was in the middle of my dreams. I did not read the chapter. What I did – in front of the book I wrote, "I Love Barbara." I don't know why I did this. But it was my book so I could say what I want.

Except that it wasn't my book. It was everybody's book, meant to be passed around from student to student, and here I sat and here, hoping to die of shame, I watched every kid in the class reading what I wrote and laughing, until it got back to the teacher. She wasn't laughing. Though maybe a slight, knowing grin. She said that it was against the rules to write inside the book, unless you are the author.

"Besides," she said, "you wrote *I Live Barbara* when you meant to say *I Love Barbara*. You get an F for spelling."

But Barbara, it turned out – all this time had a crush on me. For a time it was like in the movies but only for a time, but so nice.

22

Shabbos at the Movies

Everybody loved Jerry Lewis. Dean Martin we tolerated (not till later did I place Dean Martin as my favorite all-time entertainer alongside Frank Sinatra). Besides, Jerry Lewis was Jewish, not religious, but so what? At the time I was enrolled in a yeshiva, a Hebrew school of higher learning though there was nothing high about my learning – and this was years later in Cincinnati, Ohio, home of the Cincinnati Reds, even before The Big Red Machine. Big Klu was our hero.

Go Reds.

Back and forth we went, at that time, from Montreal to Cincinnati, until my father got the visa to get us permanently into the United States.

Nothing wrong with Montreal, great city, but it wasn't the United States.

Go Canadiens.

Chofez Chaim was the name of the yeshiva, named after a great rabbi who was famed for his piety and his strictness against evil speech, like gossip, tattling and tale bearing. Even idle talk was sinful. So I was around my early teens or pre-teens, maybe 12 or 13 and few of us were pious. We wore a kippah indoors and studied Hebrew in the morning and English in the afternoons or maybe it was the other way around.

There was a particularly great rabbi among us who later became chief rabbi of Montreal. He had an encyclopedic memory. He knew the entire Torah and most of Talmud by heart (as did my father). But nothing like that could be vouched for the rest of us, or maybe I am just speaking for myself. Actually and accidentally I did quite well, for a time, in my Hebrew studies, but in English I was terrible but somehow flunked myself upwards from one grade to the next. One time Miss Truax caught me cheating. But so was the rest of the class when it came to Latin.

I suppose some of these contemporaries of mine grew up to be great scholars and great men but I never kept in touch. But this group was all right. I liked them all and they liked me, I am pretty sure. They were so different from the kids I knew back in Montreal. They were well mannered and polite. That's how it was in Cincinnati, clean and polite and the Reds.

Decades earlier Johnny Vander Meer had pitched Major League Baseball's first and only back-to-back no-hitters and that was still the talk of the town.

I lived on Forrest Avenue with my Aunt Clara and her husband and their kids and never mind how all that happened. Long story. Clara was a doctor. She was, I was told, the first female doctor in Warsaw, Poland. I think it was Warsaw. I am sure it was Poland and I am sure that she spent two years in Auschwitz. That's where she met her husband. Not a great marriage as it turned out later on, but I did not know this.

Or maybe I was not supposed to know. There was so much I did not know. I did not even know what we were doing in Cincinnati.

That Clara did not like having my family staying with her, this I did know, but here we were anyway.

Clara had to start her career all over again because the authorities in Cincinnati refused to accept her Polish certificates. So it was tough for her.

It was tough for everybody.

Lucky for me that I did not know all the business going on all around me. We were a good family, hard-working, decent, but probably dysfunctional as all the rest.

She was beautiful, Clara was, and altogether cheerful. I did not know that she was haunted by Auschwitz. That would come out later. Later it would come out that after a half century of gaining the admiration and respect of an entire town as wife, mother, physician, philanthropist, darling of Cincinnati Society, one day something terrible happened. Something snapped. A dam of memory had collapsed and everything came roaring back.

I started getting acne around this time, when we first began living with Clara and family. I do not know why I mention this.

Except maybe that this is the time when you want to start chasing girls, so the timing for acne is terribly wrong. Which gets us to the movies where boys take girls, but when it came to Jerry Lewis it was okay to go alone. The Forrest Theater was straight down the road and about five blocks from where I lived and I took it as a route to school. So I could see the posters of what's coming next and always we waited for the next Dean Martin-Jerry Lewis movie.

All of us Chofez Chaim kids were in the same boat about this.

There it was that day, an announcement that *Jumping Jacks* was coming in two weeks. I counted the days.

Except for this: The first showing was for Saturday, the Sabbath and forbidden.

But I still counted the days. Could I wait till Sunday? No movies on Sunday. That was *their* Sabbath.

They did not have the Chofez Chaim but they did have Jesus, also watching.

No, I had to go. But I would have to do it in secret. My parents were not religious, at least not very religious (at the moment) so that was not much to worry about, and my father was back in Montreal. If I told my mother where I was going she might care or she might not care. That's how it was.

So I went. On the Sabbath. Before ducking in I made sure the coast was clear. I paid the 50 cents and tried to find a seat. Every seat in the house was taken and some were taken by my schoolmates. We pretended to see no evil. I cannot say that I enjoyed the movie. I felt sinful. I wondered what my rabbi would say about this if he ever found out.

I did not have to wonder very long. I was called into the principal's office.

"Did you go to shul on Shabbos?"

"No," I said.

"You stayed home and studied maybe?"

"No."

"So?"

"I can't remember."

"Let me remember for you. You were seen GOING TO THE MOVIES."

I nodded.

"Right?"

"Right."

"On Shabbos."

"Yes."

"Are you aware that you can be expelled for this?"

"Yes."

"So what's your explanation?"

"Explanation?"

"What can possibly be your explanation?"

"I can't think of anything."

"Try something."

"Well..."

"Well what?"

"Well it was a Jerry Lewis movie."

The rabbi gave this some thought. His expression changed and his voice turned soft.

"A Jerry Lewis movie," he said.

"Yes."

"A Jerry Lewis movie."

"Yes."

The rabbi gave this some further thought.

"Don't do it again," he said. "But all right. Go to your class."

23

Ricky Nelson
and the Radio

Please don't ask me how we got to Clark Street
when we first arrived in Montreal. I don't have all the
answers, but here we were. Frankly, I am not so sure
that Clark Street was our first address upon our
arrival from, well, the Holocaust. I think we stayed
elsewhere first for a few months. But Clark Street
was home for a number of years and it was one of
the rare times that we had a home fully to ourselves,
penniless as my parents were after spending their
entire fortune to get us out of Nazi-occupied France.

Who knew, I sure didn't, what it took, the
strength, the wisdom, the money, the connections, to
get us from there to here, mountains climbed, rivers
crossed, oceans navigated, as all the while war was
raging and a people were being burned in the ovens,
actual people in actual ovens. Can't make this up.

Who knew there was a Holocaust? No one used that term, not around me. I only knew that those people were angry and these people were scared and many people were disappearing. There was running and there was hiding and there was that time on the train, to take us to the Pyrenees, when a man in Gestapo uniform came on and started demanding papers passenger to passenger and we were at the far end and Mother froze as he began his approach and we were sunk when he came to us for my father's papers and Father coolly reached into a pocket, where he had no papers, except false papers, which meant we were doomed, and just then, that instant, the Gestapo man was called off to urgently perform another duty on the platform – and the train moved.

Sarah still says that the angel Gabriel intervened. No other explanation will do. Mother feared trains and even Montreal streetcars from that day till the end.

Back to Clark Street.

Clark Street was right at the border between the slums and the middle-class, like Esplanade, Jeanne Mance and St. Urbain where we would later settle in.

So we were not living in the slums, but close enough and dangerous enough as we were just about the only "English" among the French. We lived on the corner, making it Clark and Fairmount. Upstairs lived old Mrs. Schwartz and downstairs was the butcher shop, which I am told, by Sarah, is still there...and

Sarah says those were rats we got from the butcher. I disagree. I only saw mice.

I love my sister Sarah and we still talk about everything that happened. She fills me in on some of the details.

Sometimes we disagree, as for example, between rats and mice.

Siblings rarely share the same opinion of their parents, and on this too Sarah and I have had occasional differences.

Our father filled me up with Torah and on the wisdom of our Sages but Sarah was a girl and girls are supposed to marry and marry well.

Sarah (as opposed to me) saw the Holocaust "up close and personal" and how she turned her life into such a smash hit is a story she will tell herself.

She always was and will always be my big sister.

Back on Clark Street I hated the daytime and I loved the night. By day I had to go to school, Fairmount School, and if that wasn't bad enough I had to fight the French gangs going and coming. At night there was the radio. The radio saved my life. Imagine this – in a place far away, far from the grit and the grime of Clark Street, far from the rats or the mice, there is a place called Beverly Hills.

In that place, Beverly Hills, there were lawns and big trees and big houses and there were no worries about money.

There were no worries about anything. Nothing at all. In that place lived Ricky Nelson. He was exactly my age, except that he was born into the United

States, not France. I did not envy Ricky Nelson. But I wanted to be Ricky Nelson. I wanted his worries, like the time they went to the beach, the Nelson family, and Ricky swam out too far, so that a nickel was being reduced from his allowance for the week.

People laughed at everything he said and his mother and father doted on him. This was on the radio. All of it was on the radio.

All of America was on the radio, and in America people were always laughing. In America people were always happy.

Imagine such a place – and there it was by a flick of the dial.

Imagine a place, America, where people do not have to whisper.

So we did have a radio on Clark Street. Yes we did. I'd come home from school, usually bloodied, and wait for it to get dark. Then I'd wait for Sarah to come home from school and Sarah, for some reason, found the time and space to do her homework. None of that for me. Sarah was very beautiful and the boys were already after her, but that's another story.

My parents, sometimes, would ask Sarah to help me with some homework. She was a good, loyal sister, but I think she knew me as a lost cause.

Only about school. Otherwise we were terrific together.

Exactly eight o'clock, when everything was dark or seemed dark, we went to the radio, which was in the kitchen, atop the stove.

Why atop the stove? Because that was the nearest outlet, I suppose. As for me, I never understood why I sat on the stove to get closer to the radio.

There was no need for this. You could hear the radio even across the room. But I had to get as near as possible.

Then it all began...Jack Benny, Bob Hope, Blondie...and oh how America laughed. Me, too. I laughed right along with America. I loved *Our Miss Brooks* and of course I loved *The Adventures of Ozzie and Harriet*. These were the Nelsons, Ricky's parents, good people, such good people.

Sarah did not much care for the cowboys, but I did...Roy Rogers, Gene Autry, Hopalong Cassidy.

Somehow, my dad, or mom, got me a cowboy gun holster, just like them. One time they got me a toy pail and shovel, red and blue.

And I was on the beach with Ricky Nelson.

Sarah did like the mysteries and the detectives, but not as much as I did, like *Sam Spade, Gang Busters, Boston Blackie* and the *Fat Man*.

Sarah especially liked the French dramas and the big bands. Sometimes my mother would listen to them too. We made it loud enough for her to hear. I think I saw her crying about that one time, as I suppose it reminded her of the good days in Toulouse, France when she had been rich and had attended and even hosted all those parties where people danced.

Mostly though Sarah and I stayed tuned for the comedy shows. How far was Beverly Hills?

Not far at all.

That is why I climbed so far up the stove. I did this because the closer I got to the radio, maybe inside the radio, the closer I got to Ricky Nelson and his America.

24

Kindergarten Is Not for Children

There are boys and there are girls and let's face it, boys know nothing about girls. We love them, we adore them, we honor them, but they are a strange race. We don't know what they want, exactly as Freud said, so if he did not know, the rest of us have no clue. They are inscrutable.

The mystery of it all begins in kindergarten, at least that is where it began for me. So at the moment we made our entrance into Montreal I was thrown into a kindergarten. Just like that I was among fellow five or six-year-olds, boys and those other people, all so sweet. Immediately I found myself blushing. I did not know these people, the boys or the girls, and I did not even know their language, English, nor did I know the teacher's language, also English.

We played games and drew pictures and everything had to be explained to me twice.

I made it a point to keep my mouth shut. I was
afraid people would giggle, especially the girls. (The
problem starts early.)

Most likely the kids and the teacher took me for a
mute. I liked to play house. There was a table for this
with toy cups, dishes, knives and forks. I ran to this
table at playtime and there was one particular girl I
wanted as a mate and usually she complied and
smiled but I said nothing or mostly nothing, for I did
know a few words and maybe even more than a few.
Her name was Teresa.

The fear, the panic had me from the moment my
mother took me by the hand and enrolled me.

The fear was naptime. This took place from noon
until two and we were all supposed to cuddle into
bunks and nap and be quiet. But suppose...

Suppose I had to go to the bathroom, as I knew I
would. What would I say? What language understands
this?

How do I say this without humiliating myself?
The girls were sure to laugh. I only knew this –
pee pee.

I hoped to attract the teacher's attention so that
only she would find me shameful and ridiculous.

From what I could tell, nobody else ever had to go
to the bathroom. Only me. If they did, and they didn't,
they never said pee pee.

So I tried to get the teacher ahead of time to ask her what is to be done in an emergency, but there was no way to catch her attention.

Certainly I could not raise an arm and speak out about this publicly, not even in proper English and most certainly not in halting English.

"Naptime," said the teacher.

The girl I played house with, Teresa, whispered something to the teacher.

"But first," said the teacher, eyeing me specially and kindly, "it's bathroom time."

Teresa...my first friend in the New World.

Escape from Mount Moriah

25

A Slight Kidnapping

Park Avenue was the Fifth Avenue or the Avenue des Champs-Elysées of Montreal. Maybe I am wrong about this. Maybe there were fancier streets. But that is how it appeared to me. My father even had a shop there for a while, among the bright lights, but that is another story. So along Park Avenue as it approached the foot of the mountain, this is where people promenaded.

To promenade was a big deal. This was where you met people, especially your own people, your landsmen. So it wasn't about taking a walk. It was a social event. Sometimes there were hundreds of us. Or so it seemed. The parents would walk and sometimes they would stop and chat. The kids tagged along.

It was about grace and ritual, as it had been done in Europe. These were mostly refugees. Sometimes it seemed that everybody came from Poland.

All were spiffed out in their fineries.

The promenade would begin family by family and then it would split off with men walking with men and women walking with women.

I hated everything about this. I wanted to be with my friends. This whole business was for adults, so why bother me?

Who are these people?

Some were in fact from the same places that my father and mother knew, in Poland or France or wherever. It seemed important to know names and places and some came from that place where they put tattoos on your arms. There were quite a few people like that and sometimes there was hugging and kissing and weeping.

I did not know what was going on except that I had to keep walking as my mom and dad kept promenading.

Quite a few times my mother ran to someone, or someone ran to my mother and they began talking and crying.

I knew that much information was being sought and exchanged... Auschwitz, Treblinka, Bergen-Belsen...strange places.

Many people on the promenade came from Warsaw or Lodz for some reason.

I wanted to play baseball.

But my mother had me by the arm, and tightly so. Her grip on me was terrible. I tried to let go but then she'd hold me even tighter. The signal was clear. I was to stay with her and not wander off. This made no sense, except that it was the same for those other kids who were forced to tag along.

I asked Sarah about this and she said never mind, I wouldn't understand. Frankly, I think she was spared the entire ordeal.

I think she was allowed to be with her girlfriends. She was older, after all.

Although, I do think my mother encouraged her to come along to meet some boys. Sarah would have none of this.

So it was just me on these promenades.

I heard the word Hitler quite a lot. People spat when they said that name.

So we walked and this day I managed to let go. In an instant, amid the swarm, I was cut loose. A woman in tears grabbed me and tried to run off with me.

"He is mine," yelled the woman when my mother reached the scene of my abduction, and she was equally hysterical – and I do mean hysterical.

I found myself being tugged back and forth.

My mother shrieked. She hollered for my father.

"You stole my baby," said the woman, howling.

"What?"

"You stole my child. This is my son."

My father appeared.

"They took him from me in Buchenwald and they gave him to you. This is my son."

He got me back from the firm clutches of the woman, but it was a fight.

Fearful of my father and his display of violent temper, the woman ran off empty-handed but still howling, "They stole my son."

That was the end of this promenade and I do not remember promenading ever again.

26

Trouble
at the Border

Please remember that where I came from there was nothing like America, even if you were living in Canada.

America was the big leagues. The rest – anywhere in the world? Minor league. Except for hockey, of course. America had Babe Ruth. But Canada had Maurice "Rocket" Richard. Even more – America had the *New York Yankees*. But Canada had the glorious *Montreal Canadiens* and for a while the two were head to head compiling the most number of championships.

But everything about America glittered, truly the beacon.

So onward we go to America when I was about 16 or 18 and forgive me if I can't remember. It makes no difference except that I had to share with America what it was like in Times Square New Year's Eve. We heard it on the radio and we saw it on television, at that moment when the clock struck a new year, and if you were not in Times Square you were no place.

The cheers...the crowds...the joy...the fun...and the parties?...and the girls? Maybe I would meet someone. Maybe I would never have to go back.

I had to go and I went.

Not so simple. First I had to get some money. I got some. But only for a bus ticket and some food.

Then I had to leave the house without telling my parents, which would suggest that I was 16. (At 18 I was mostly on my own.) I would have to run away. This would come as no surprise as I ran away from home quite frequently. So I timed it to be in New York just when the hoopla began.

The bus was cheapest so that is why I took the bus. I preferred trains. The trip was long but thrilling. After all, think of the destination. So here we are and it's about 10 p.m., only two hours before the greatest spectacle on earth and here I am in Times Square waiting. Nothing so far. But just being here is extraordinary.

If I thought Park Avenue in Montreal was the headquarters of the world – look at this! Of course I had been to New York a few times before, but never alone, so it was new all over again. Something about the people. The way they walk. The way they laugh and how they never have to whisper, never in America. They walk those big steps, head high, arms wide, as if they own the world – and they do!

It was snowing and it was freezing, so as much as I wanted to walk around and do some exploring, I decided to get a cup of coffee instead. On some side street I walked into a small, dingy restaurant for a cup of coffee. The man behind the counter, wearing a filthy apron, said, "Yeah?" I said, "Coffee, please."

The word "please" was obviously nothing he had ever heard before so he gave me a second look, as did a tired waitress down the end on a stool smoking a cigarette. I got the coffee, drank it down, and handed the man a dollar. He looked it over. "What's this?" he said.

"A dollar bill," I said.

"Never seen anything like it," he said.

"It's Canadian."

"Can't accept this."

"Excuse me?"

"We only take American money."

"I did not know this."

"So now you know. Got any American money?"

"No."

"Some places take Canadian money. Not here, kid. All right."

He let me go without washing the dishes. But this was a wrinkle. But he did say other places take Canadian money so there was no reason to be concerned.

I would worry about it later.

So now it was getting close to midnight and this time Times Square was humming. First came hundreds, and soon thousands, me in the middle of it all. People were laughing and screaming even before the ball went down, only everybody else had a partner and I was alone but that made no difference. I was happy. Every girl had a partner, so I would have to skip that part.

But I was here, wasn't I?

I would have a million stories to tell back home.

Now people – a million of them – started counting, and the ball started coming down and it was bedlam.

In that instant, I lost something. I lost the thrill. I asked myself, what is the big deal? Is it the ball? So what? It's a ball. Is it that, in an instant, there's a new year coming? Who says the new year will be better than the old year? That never happens. One year is as good as the next or as bad as the next and sometimes even worse. I know this. This much I know. So what is this all about? Made no sense. This can't be everything.

Surely after the ball lands, that's when the parties will begin, and I am sure to be invited. I may meet that girl, after all. There were plenty of girls.

One of them must have been lacking a boyfriend.

But after the ball came down and people sang that song, after that, people dispersed. In a flash the streets emptied. I was alone in Times Square.

But wait. Here's a happy crowd heading for some ballroom – Guy Lombardo? I knew, from television, that on New Year's there were big parties all around the town.

So I followed all these happy, drunken people, ready to party. But it was the entrance to the subways. That's where they were going.

That's it?

That's it.

Yes, that's it.

I was starved. I needed to eat something, fast. In those days I had dizzy spells if I went too long without nourishment. I tried a big restaurant, like Lindy's.

I said, "Do you take Canadian money?"

"Canadian?"

Is Canada really such a foreign country around here? Are we not neighbors?

"Yes, Canadian."

"No. You'll have to get it changed."

"Where, please?"

He said there's a place on 44th that changes money.

"I'll be back," I said.

"Good luck."

I went over to that place that changes money. But the sign said, "Closed for the holidays."

Bad luck.

I waited four hours for the bus to get me back to Montreal and good thing that I had bought a round trip ticket.

But it was a bad thing at the border. The bus was stopped and I was taken into an office for questioning.

"Why were you in New York?"

"For a New Year party."

"Anything else?"

"Nothing else."

"Are you sure?"

"I am sure."

"You went alone?"

"Yes, Sir."

"Isn't that strange?"

"I don't know."

"So now where do you want to go?"

"Home. Montreal."

"Well, you have a problem."

I had no proof.

I had no proof that I was a Canadian citizen and I had no proof that I was an American citizen.

I was a man without a country.

These were not Gestapo. But they were men in uniform.

They thought I was a runaway. Maybe a criminal. Maybe a smuggler. Maybe a spy?

They gave me a room in some corner with a cot to get some sleep while they figured me out. But I was too scared for sleep.

Does this end with me never to get back home? Does this finish with me never to be anywhere – stuck between two countries?

I was terrified.

In the middle of the night a soldier came in and said I could go. There was a Montreal bus outside waiting.

He escorted me.

"Did you enjoy your New Year's celebration in New York?"

"Oh yes. Unforgettable."

Escape from Mount Moriah

27

The Pineapple Revolt

There was only fear on this ship, and pineapples, several hundred passengers, a million pineapples.

We were on the Serpa Pinto, on the high seas destined from Hitler to FDR, or whoever would take us in. FDR refused.

So we were headed for Philadelphia, and after that, who knew?

But along with the rest of the huddled men, women and children on board, we were the few who had managed to escape.

We were free.

Except for the German U-Boats.

They still wanted us.

We could be stopped at any moment. Sunk. Taken back. Or shot on sight.

The Serpa Pinto had sailed from Lisbon, Portugal. Somehow (yes, long story) a deal was done and three voyages were arranged to transport the survivors.

We were on the first trip, an adventure from beginning to end. People knew that there were German torpedo boats and submarines on patrol, so there was no rejoicing. This was 1944.

The ship had to do summersaults and zigzags to avoid being stopped or hit, so if you were prone to seasickness you got seasick. I threw up a few times.

I did not know exactly what was going on as I was but four years old. But I sensed the tension. These were people, like my parents, who'd left behind everything.

The nausea was with me throughout and I searched for smiles and laughter and there was some of that among the passengers, but not much.

We were the uprooted. The world had used us and toyed with us and even now, anything could be done to us.

We had no powers. We had no rights.

Earlier, Hitler had used another ship, the Saint Louis, to prove that the entire world was in cahoots with him. The Saint Louis was turned back from every port – including the United States – and virtually all the refugee passengers were sent back to the welcoming arms of the Gestapo.

So, as my mother used to say, "We were the lucky ones."

Later, and only a few years later, Jews would prove themselves to be mighty warriors.

But not at this moment, as the ship tossed and heaved.

This wasn't like cruising on the Queen Mary.

As the ship drew closer to some New Land, people began to shed their helplessness and some even grew bold.

"Why so many pineapples?"

I guessed as much myself. What's with the pineapples? Everywhere, pineapples. Pineapples for breakfast, for lunch, for dinner and for snacks.

More than the seasickness, this was the cause of my nausea.

Pineapples are good. There is nothing more harmless than a pineapple. It is nourishment, after all. But so many?

I can't remember the exact moment, but a mutiny began – against pineapples.

We had no army against the Nazis. But we could fight the pineapples. Weren't they just as ubiquitous as the Nazis?

Everywhere you turned – here was a Nazi.

Now everywhere you turned – here was a pineapple.

Therefore, the pineapples were Nazis.

As before, we were outnumbered by them, but this time we had a strategy.

We would toss them overboard.

The word was passed and all the men and even all the women and even all the kids, that included me, gathered up all the pineapples, tossed them on deck and then began hurling them into the ocean – with fury and with curses. We were determined to let not a single pineapple survive.

So we arrived in Philadelphia, beaten, broken, but not defeated.

28

Waiting for America

I wish I knew where this happened and when this happened, but it happened. I do know that this was the final step, the final procedure for getting us into America. Temporary permits – these were normally available to my father to get us going forth and back. But this was to be the real thing, the visa, the permanent visa to get us in to stay.

Was it a checkpoint of some sort? Had to be more than that. Because we were in a place with high walls and big pictures showing images of American presidents. Most likely this was a consulate and even more likely this was an ambassador's office. The four of us were sitting in a waiting room, as were other couples and families, all waiting nervously, but none as nervous as my mother and father.

Could go either way. We were obviously awaiting a verdict; this way was America, that way meant being sent back.

One man was to be the judge. He held our life in his hands. This was the ambassador.

But something was wrong. I was not being told what, but something was wrong. When waiting for judgment, something can always go wrong. But this was something in particular. We may have been waiting only an hour, but it seemed like hours. We sat there and watched people, official people, going into one door and out the next.

Each time my father and mother jumped. Was it for us? Was there news? Had the judgment been made? Which man or woman would bring the news?

They all seemed so official and so grim. There were no smiles, only a door opening and a door closing.

Would it be this man or would it be that man? Was this the ambassador or was that the ambassador?

There was fright all around.

Finally a door opened – it was all about doors opening and shutting – a man stepped up, stepped up to us, unsmiling. My mother froze.

He wore a tag on his lapel, but it was unclear if this was the ambassador himself.

Was this it?

An ocean crossed for this one single moment.

Are we to be welcomed or are we to be expelled.

In Kafka's courts, first they prosecuted and executed; after that they heard testimony.

Were our papers in order? Always papers. One flaw in those papers and you were sunk.

Show me, said Robespierre – show me 20 words written by any man, and I will find some reason to hang him.

"Your son," said the man.

Me?

My sister Sarah had to help translate. My father understood English well enough (not my mother) but he was so frightened...

"My son?" said my father.

"Yes, are you aware that he has an irregular heartbeat...and that this could prevent you and your family from entering the United States?"

Sarah translated all that for my mother and father. They conferred.

Finally, Father said that yes, back in France I had scarlet fever. But why should that...

The man turned and left.

Was this the end?

"Is this the end?" Mother asked Father.

"Shh," said Father.

"Is this the end?" Mother wanted to know. "If so..."

Yes, if so, what? Where?

"Wait," said Father. "We wait."

So we sat waiting...and we may well be doomed...all on account of me. Until that moment I had not known about the scarlet fever.

Now I knew. *They* knew when they had given each of us a physical. This was required of all refugees.

We may well be waiting for nothing. Had the verdict already been announced?

The man had not even told us to keep waiting. He simply turned to another door, another office...and more of them kept going from this office to that office.

All of them so tall...so different from those of us who were waiting.

So our papers were in order after all. But not for me. I was not in order.

Another man stepped out of an office and walked up to us and again my mother turned pale.

"Your son may have to undergo another examination," said the man, and then walked away into another room.

"What could they find except more of the same," Mother whispered to Father.

"We don't know. We don't know anything."

All my fault.

Sarah caressed me.

"It's not your fault," she said.

We waited. More doors. More rooms. The same people and different people walking from here to there, doors always shut.

"Where do we go?" Mother whispered, already prepared for the worst.

A woman steps out from an office.

"Follow me," she says.

We follow her. Mother – strong as she is; this woman climbed a mountain! – needs help to get to her feet.

A tall man, the tallest of them all, is on the telephone. This is the ambassador. We wait for him to finish.

"It's okay," he says. "Welcome to the United States."

That is what he says. He says, "Welcome to the United States."

Escape from Mount Moriah

Epilogue

The Cardinal

Is it ever too late to give gratitude? Must there be an anniversary? But time is running out, so every day is an anniversary.

On July 10, 1942, The Roundup of Paris had already begun. On orders from the Gestapo, the French police began knocking on doors and swiftly some 13,000 Jews were whisked to the transit depot Vélodrome d'Hiver. They were permitted a blanket, a shirt and a pair of socks in addition to what they were wearing. There was no air-conditioning.

Many were dragged from their homes, their children tagging along, baffled and weeping.

They were told that they were simply being "relocated," but all were destined for Auschwitz.

But that was Paris, and this was Toulouse – the Free Zone.

Toulouse was the most Catholic of all cities. Yet Christians and Jews lived together in harmony. The mood changed when Hitler arrived. Sarah's classmate and best friend Incarnacion one day called her a "dirty Jew." Was that the day she saw the handwriting on the wall?

"No," says Sarah, now writing her memoir about all that, so many years later. Her father Noah saw it coming when family members began disappearing.

"Even in Toulouse?"

Yes, even in Toulouse. "Germans were directing traffic," she says, "so they were everywhere."

Bags packed from day one, it was time to escape. Noah was in touch with the French underground and through other connections he saved his family. Every step he took – Nazi terror all around – could have been the end, but he risked it all to save others as well. To every man comes that day to prove himself a man and when that day fell to Noah, he seized it with both arms. He was a hero.

The world had shut its doors. Prior to the establishment of Israel, there was no place to turn except to righteous Christians.

Like Father LaRoche.

This was the priest who sheltered Jews and who opened all the channels for the getaway across the Pyrenees, risking his own life.

"The people who saved us were in the same danger as we were," recalls Sarah. "Many were killed."

The French were informers against their Jewish neighbors and traitors against Christianity.

But there were exceptions, quite noble and notable.

To them, gratitude must be given.

"We don't know their names," says Sarah. "That hurts."

Yet we do know Father LaRoche, and still another name shines through the darkness - Cardinal Jules-Géraud Saliège, the Archbishop of Toulouse.

A month after the Roundup of Paris, seeing what's in store for Toulouse as well, Saliège wrote a letter of protest in which he declared, "Jews are our brothers." In other words, do not touch God's anointed. At his insistence, the document was distributed and read throughout the diocese.

In 1969, Jerusalem's Yad Vashem honored Saliège as Righteous among the Nations, with this inscription that reads in part:

"Overnight, the document became a manifesto; hundreds of thousands of copies were circulated by members of the Resistance throughout France. Historians consider Saliège's protest vastly influential in the abrupt turnabout in French public opinion regarding the [anti-Semitic] Vichy regime."

Moreover, "Saliège instructed the clergymen and nuns to hide Jews, particularly children."

Sarah was among those children destined to be hidden. But her father Noah proclaimed, "We will live together or die together." So began the perilous exodus from France for the few. The many who were trapped and murdered are numbered in excess of 70,000.

We will never know how many lives were saved thanks to Cardinal Saliège.

Was it Saliège himself who, in better days, brought chocolates for Sarah, and studied Torah with Noah? Yes, together the rabbi and the priest studied the Hebrew Bible.

Surely it was Father LaRoche. But chances are that it was also the Archbishop himself.

To some, this is historic. To others, like Sarah, this is personal. Surely it was personal to a number of valiant priests and nuns, and to our father, Noah.

Made in the USA
San Bernardino, CA
23 April 2019